# The Welfare State in Capitalist Society

**Studies in international social policy and welfare**

Series Editors:    Professor Stewart MacPherson, University of
Papua New Guinea
Professor James Midgley, Louisiana State
University

*Other titles available:*

*The Crisis in Welfare: An International Perspective on Social
Services and Social Work.* Brian Munday (editor)

*Modern Welfare States: A Comparative View of Trends and
Prospects.* Robert Friedmann, Neil Gilbert and Moshe Sherer
(editors)

*Comparative Social Policy and the Third World.* Stewart
MacPherson and James Midgley

*Five Hundred Million Children: Child Welfare in the Third World.*
Stewart MacPherson

# The Welfare State in Capitalist Society

## Policies of Retrenchment and Maintenance in Europe, North America and Australia

**Ramesh Mishra**

*York University, Ontario*

# HARVESTER WHEATSHEAF

New York   London   Toronto   Sydney   Tokyo   Singapore

First published 1990 by
Harvester Wheatsheaf
66 Wood Lane End, Hemel Hempstead
Hertfordshire HP2 4RG
A division of
Simon & Schuster International Group

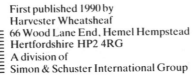

Typeset in 10/12 pt Times
by Keyset Composition, Colchester

Printed and bound in Great Britain by
Billing and Sons Limited, Worcester

---

British Library Cataloguing in Publication Data

---

Mishra, Ramesh
  The welfare state in capitalist society: policies of retrenchment and
  maintenance in Europe, North America and Australia. – (Studies in
  international social policy and welfare; v. 5)
  1. Welfare state
  I. Title   II. Series
  361.65

  ISBN 0-7450-0049-5
  ISBN 0-7450-0211-0 pbk

---

1 2 3 4 5   94 93 92 91 90

To the memory of Sumita

# Contents

# Series editors' preface

This is the fifth volume in Harvester Wheatsheaf's *Studies in International Social Policy and Welfare* series. Committed to the advocacy of a global perspective in social policy research, the series seeks to publish work which transcends developments in specific countries. By abstracting general trends and issues from local experiences, scholars gain powerful insights into phenomena that cannot be adequately interpreted within the framework of domestic realities. Ramesh Mishra's new book, *The Welfare State in Capitalist Society*, is a prime example of this genre, and of the advantages of a methodological approach that draws extensively on comparative material. His analysis of the fortunes of the modern welfare state in conditions of economic and ideological adversity is able to generate propositions of significance because it sweeps masterfully over developments on three continents, distilling a multiplicity of discrete domestic events into a coherent, comprehensible account. In this way, Mishra not only fosters a deeper understanding of the forces that impinge on modern welfare systems, shaping their character and future, but also contributes to the growth of social policy as an academic subject. As social policy ventures increasingly into unexplored comparative terrains, its scholarly standing is enhanced. The series is committed to the task of widening the subject's perspective, and Professor Mishra's book serves it well. We are proud to publish the work of this distinguished scholar.

Stewart MacPherson
Professor of Sociology
University of Papua New Guinea

James Midgley
Dean of the School of Social Work
Louisiana State University

# Acknowledgements

Dr Keith Banting and Dr Pat Evans read the book in its draft stage and made detailed comments. My grateful thanks to both. Priscilla Harding managed the task of processing the various drafts of the book with consummate ease and good cheer. She also edited the draft chapters and made substantive comments on the manuscript. Her major contribution in the preparation of this book is gratefully acknowledged. A grant from the Social Sciences and Humanities Research Council of Canada facilitated data collection and enabled me to visit some of the countries discussed in this book. My thanks to colleagues in Canada and abroad who gave generously of their time to discuss this study with me and helped me understand the national contexts of social policy. Finally, thanks are due to my publishers, Harvester Wheatsheaf, for turning a blind eye to my frequent disregard of deadlines. The shortcomings of the book naturally remain my responsibility.

# Introduction

It is more than fifteen years since the first oil-price shock sent inflation soaring and gave rise to a new economic phenomenon in the West – stagflation. It is over ten years since the first neo-conservative government came to power in Britain on the basis of an ideology that repudiated the post-war consensus around a mixed economy and the welfare state. As we enter the 1990s, neo-conservative regimes remain in office in Britain and in the United States. However, contrary to what many people on the left feared and many on the right (and perhaps the far left) hoped, the welfare state has not been dismantled by neo-conservatives. Much of the building stands intact even though cracks are beginning to show, upkeep and maintenance have been minimal and the furnishings are beginning to look shabby. At the other end of the spectrum, Swedish social democracy also remains in power, wedded as much as in the past to the policy of full employment and social welfare. Again, contrary to what many had expected both on the far left and the right, social democracy as a political compromise has not been undermined. This is particularly true of 'corporatist' social democracy as practised in countries like Sweden and Austria. What is more, public support for mainstream universal services remains strong in all Western countries. Much of this suggests continuity and stability and lends credence to the idea that the welfare state has become an irreversible development. What, then, are we to make of the 'crisis' that seemed to have hit the Keynesian welfare state in the mid-1970s? Has the storm blown over and are we once again sailing in calm waters? Is it business as usual, with only a little less cash to go around, and rather more modest expectations for the future as far as social welfare is concerned? And if not, then what *has* changed? What is the state of the welfare state as we enter the 1990s?

This book is an attempt to answer these admittedly rather large questions. Put simply, the recent history of the welfare state is seen here in terms of three phases: pre-crisis (before 1973), crisis (the mid- to late 1970s), and post-crisis (the 1980s and beyond). The pre-crisis phase was represented by a relatively stable Keynes–Beveridge paradigm. The crisis phase saw a sharp decline in the credibility of the Keynesian welfare state as a paradigm and the emergence of neo-conservatism. The post-crisis phase began with the election of neo-conservative governments pledged to break with the objectives and methods of the Keynesian welfare state. The post-crisis phase therefore appears to be one in which the ideological spectrum in social welfare policy has widened, albeit mainly in a rightward direction. Neo-conservatism and social-democratic corporatism appear to be two fairly distinct responses to the predicament of welfare capitalism in the 1970s, the former seeking to retrench the welfare state, the latter seeking to defend it. But do these two responses differ chiefly in their political ideology and rhetoric or are substantial differences in policy and outcome also involved? This book argues that the latter is the case and that these two types of regime represent different clusters of values and interests associated with major class groupings in capitalist society – capital and labour. In short, substantial questions of policies, values and social consequences are involved. In practical terms these two types of regime represent the ideological limits within which the contemporary drama of social welfare is being played out. This follows on the argument outlined in my book, *The Welfare State in Crisis*, which saw the rise of neo-conservatism as the response from the right and the corporatist 'integrated' approach of social-democratic welfare states as the most effective response on the left. The present work, which examines these two social policy models in action in some detail, can thus be seen as a sequel to *The Welfare State in Crisis*.

Chapter 1 outlines the emergence of neo-conservative and social-democratic corporatist responses in the post-1973 period, seen as representing the objectives of welfare state retrenchment and maintenance, respectively. It also sketches the theoretical perspective of the book, which revolves around the notions of class, crisis, ideology and policy. Chapter 2 looks at the strategy of retrenchment in action in two countries, the United States and the United Kingdom, and, in light of the findings, considers the argument that the welfare state has become irreversible. Chapter 3 looks at the strategy of maintenance at work in two countries, Sweden and Austria, and highlights the differences in policies and their outcome between these countries and neo-conservative regimes. It considers briefly various criticisms levelled against social corporatism by the left, notably that it is biased in favour of organized producer interests. Chapter 4 looks at Canada and Australia, two countries which have sought in recent years to emulate the strategies of the new right and social corporatism, respectively. The aim of this chapter is to extend the range of available evidence on the working of the two approaches beyond the classic cases of the United Kingdom, the United States, Sweden and Austria. Chapter 5 summarizes the results of the country studies and considers their implications for the main argument of the book. It offers a critical review of some of the main interpretations of the welfare state in light of the arguments and evidence presented in the earlier chapters. Finally, it suggests new analytical perspectives for a better understanding of current developments in social welfare.

# 1

# The end of post-war consensus: strategies of retrenchment and maintenance

The post-war consensus around the mixed economy and the welfare state, to which almost all advanced Western countries subscribed to a greater or lesser extent, weakened a good deal in the 1970s. The reasons for this breakdown were primarily 'material' rather than 'ideational'. True, in the United States from the late 1960s social scientists and philosophers on the right had begun denigrating the Great Society reforms and were cultivating disillusionment with social engineering itself.[1] More generally, neo-conservative philosophers had begun to counterpose the idea of the minimal state against the liberal Rawlsian notion of social justice which implied a larger role for the government in economic and social matters.[2] In the United Kingdom, it should be noted, a comparable groundswell of right-wing ideas did not appear until the mid-1970s or even later. On both sides of the Atlantic, however, what enabled neo-conservative ideas to gain a hearing and what eventually created a market for them was the change in material conditions – in short, the advent of stagflation. The combination of inflation and recession was something new and not easily amenable to Keynesian solutions. As economic conditions deteriorated in the West from about the mid-1970s and failed to recover or return to anything like a 'normal' situation, general confidence in the mixed economy and the welfare state pretty much evaporated. Above all, the apparently benevolent role of the state in managing the economy and in financing an ever growing range of social services came under direct attack. This much is history.[3]

What is important from the viewpoint of this book is the fact that the neo-Keynesian orthodoxy of the post-war years has not been replaced thus far by a new orthodoxy – whether of the right, centre or left. No new 'settlement', or even its lineaments, are in sight. Rather, we have a situation where regimes have responded in a variety of ways to economic problems. On the one hand, we have seen neo-conservative governments in the United Kingdom and the United States apparently determined to carve out a new path for their nations – one which allows more scope for private enterprise and the market and reduces the scope of the state in respect of its economic and social activity. On the other hand, we have the social-democratic corporatist approach (which for convenience we will refer to as 'social-corporatist'), for example in Austria and Sweden, whose main feature is concerted action involving major economic interests and the state, based on a broad consensus on the maintenance of the mixed economy and the welfare state. At the same time it should be pointed out that this is not a new departure in the manner of neo-conservatism. These countries have been following a more or less social-corporatist route since about the late 1960s. However, the significance of this particular approach to managing welfare capitalism has become much more apparent since the collapse of Keynesianism and the resurgence of the New Right.[4] Thus neo-conservatism and social corporatism may be seen as two distinct responses to the problems and difficulties of welfare capitalism in the 1970s and beyond. Leaving aside purely ideological responses (i.e. Marxism) to the problems of welfare capitalism, the situation in which Western welfare states now find themselves could be summed up as follows. On the right there is the model of neo-conservatism, with its rhetoric and ideology of retrenching social welfare, relying on the private sector and market forces for economic growth and for the provision of various human services. Its objective is to reduce substantially the 'welfare' element of welfare capitalism. On the left, in a practical and not merely theoretical sense, we have the model of social corporatism which has refused to abandon the goals of the post-war welfare state, notably full employment, economic growth and social welfare.

As far as social welfare is concerned, the former might be described as the strategy and policy of *retrenching*, the latter that of *maintaining* the welfare state. These two extremes, so to speak, can be seen as the end points of a continuum on which most other welfare states of our times can be situated with respect to their objectives and policies. True, over the last two decades a variety of ideas and social movements relevant to issues of social welfare have arisen which cut across the left–right and public–private divide. These include ecological and other forms of 'post-industrial' as well as feminist movements. But so far these remain somewhat tangential to the ideology and politics of welfare in Western democracies.

It is one thing, however, to profess an ideology of welfare, whether of retrenchment or maintenance. It is quite another to be able to practise it successfully. Thus the Reagan administration came to power with a promise to reduce the government deficit, indeed, to cut back public expenditure and eventually to balance the budget. In the event, under Reagan the budget deficit soared to historically high levels. In the United Kingdom, too, the advent of the Thatcher government saw a rise rather than a fall in social expenditure (see page 34 below). The framework of universal social services, notably education, health care and income security, has also remained largely intact in both the United States and the United Kingdom, notwithstanding neo-conservative rhetoric of privatization and retrenchment of social welfare. On the other hand, social-democratic regimes such as Sweden and Austria, while upholding the principle of collective responsibility for the welfare of the nation, have in practice been obliged to trim social expenditure and accept higher levels of unemployment. These conditions have lent considerable support to a new thesis of convergence or rather structural constraint, which argues that the welfare state is irreversible, right-wing rhetoric notwithstanding.[5] Is the New Right, then, more bark rather than bite as far as the welfare state is concerned? If so, by the same token the relevance of social corporatism also weakens in that under different ideological flags flown by regimes the reality of social welfare remains pretty much the same. This is an important thesis, and a major interest of this work is to examine this proposition in light of policies and their consequences in the United States and the United Kingdom under neo-conservative regimes and in Sweden and Austria under social-corporatist regimes. While these two pairs of countries can be seen as the most redoubtable exponents of the contrasting approaches we have identified, two other countries, Canada and Australia, will also be examined as candidate members of one or the other of these two policy 'clubs'.

In Canada the Progressive Conservative Party swept to power in

1984 with a landslide majority. Once in office the new government showed a clear propensity for a neo-conservative approach to social welfare. Faced with strong protest, however, it retreated. Does this support the 'irreversibility' thesis or is it the case that, instead of a frontal assault, there is a strategy of piecemeal retrenchment at work in Canada? The question assumes greater importance with the election of Conservatives to a second term of office in 1988 and the subsequent passage of the free trade agreement with the United States.

About a year before Canada elected a Conservative government, Australia moved in the other direction. There a Labour government took office whose economic and social strategy was based on an 'Accord' with the trade unions and a tripartite approach – in short, a form of social corporatism. Indeed, a Labour government in Britain had embarked on a similar 'Social Contract' which broke down irretrievably, sweeping Margaret Thatcher to power.[6] In light of the failure of the social-corporatist approach in Britain, Australia's attempt to use it as a base for harmonizing the economic and social objectives of welfare capitalism is of considerable interest. At the time of writing (1989) the Australian Accord still holds. Mirroring Thatcher's record, the Labour government in Australia is now also in its third term of office. Has Australian social corporatism been a success? What policies has the social-democratic regime in Australia followed and with what consequences? Does the Australian experience support the view that social corporatism offers an effective means of the defence of the welfare state? In short, the diffusion and operation of neo-conservative and social-corporatist models beyond the four 'hard-core' countries is also a matter of considerable interest especially from the vantage point of the ideology and practice of social welfare in English-speaking countries.

No doubt social welfare institutions and practices of neo-conservative and social-corporatist regimes are similar in many ways. But the interest of this work lies more in their *differences*. This interest stems from a theoretical as well as a value standpoint. More generally, it is an approach against determinisms of various sorts and in support of the possibility of choice and change. Far too long in the history of post-war social sciences, especially politics and sociology, global determinism of one kind or another – whether Marxist or otherwise – about social development has occupied centre-stage. The variations, the choices and the options available, even if within limits, have on the whole been played down. From the standpoint of social welfare, in particular, these differences matter a great deal. For policy choices have quite direct and far-reaching value implications for the well-being of individuals. What the breakdown of the Keynesian welfare state paradigm has underlined above all is the possibility of variations; of choice and change in the social organization of industrialized capitalist societies. This is a lesson driven home forcefully by the 'counter-revolution' of the right. But what sort of choice and what kind of change? From the viewpoint of this book, this is the crux of the matter. The policy responses and the models we consider (neo-conservative and social-corporatist) and the countries we examine can together be seen as so many social experiments relevant to the future of social welfare and capitalist democracies. Will neo-conservatism – with its promise of economic growth, higher productivity and voluntary initiative with respect to economic and social welfare – be triumphant and increasingly attract voters and nations to itself? Will this happen because it is able to deliver on its promises or rather from a sense that there are no other options within a capitalist society? Alternatively, will nations such as Sweden and Austria – with their integrated approach, which considers economic and social policy issues as interrelated and which seeks to work through a tripartite form of decision-making – offer an attractive framework within which the essentials of the post-war welfare state may be maintained and perhaps consolidated? Or again will it turn out to be the case, as the 'irreversibility' thesis implies, that, in effect, the structure of the welfare state will remain intact with only minor impairments and differences? These problems have a theoretical as well as a practical interest and various national experiments have an importance that may well extend beyond their boundaries. There may be scope here for 'lesson-learning'.

It is important, however, to acknowledge that policies are made and options exercised within a national context. While social scientists as far apart in time and in theoretical stance as Marx and Titmuss agree that nations can and should learn from each other – whether positive or negative lessons – it also remains true that the history of nation-states is characterized by a great deal of cultural and institutional insularity which resists change. Moreover, the structural and cultural configuration that goes to make up a nation-state in its historical continuity makes the nature of 'problems' peculiarly national. By the same token, it makes certain kinds of change and direction more feasible than others. Even so, general models of social organization have several uses. At one level they have a 'demonstration effect' in that they show that certain kinds of social arrangements are feasible and therefore, in principle at any rate, available to all nations. At another level their historical existence and more or less successful functioning induce a critical attitude or at least a comparative frame of reference towards those social arrangements which constitute the status quo.[7]

Comparison implies evaluation, which in turn suggests the possibility of choice and change. The history of social welfare provides many examples of diffusion. In the late nineteenth and early twentieth century, Bismarckian social insurance measures had a considerable 'demonstration effect' not only in European countries, but also in the United States. However distant politically the authoritarian German state was from the liberal-democratic polities of Britain and the United States, there is no denying the impact of Bismarck's pioneering social insurance scheme. Its diffusion was undoubtedly piecemeal and gradual, but clearly there were lessons to be learned and they were learned by nations very different in politics and culture from Germany.[8] Nearer our time, the emergence of the Keynes–Beveridge welfare state in post-war Britain also had a 'demonstration effect' at least on English-speaking countries, although in its comprehensiveness, institutional features and timing it was a peculiarly British phenomenon. Clearly, the influence is often indirect. 'Diffusion' is not simply a matter of *importing* institutions *in toto*. Thus the Beveridge Report inspired the Marsh Report in Canada, which may be described as the blueprint for the Canadian welfare state. But it took Canada more than twenty years to translate some of the principal recommendations of the Marsh Report into social welfare policy.[9] Today it appears that neo-conservative and social-corporatist approaches to policy-making may be candidates for diffusion. A major objective of this book is to compare these two approaches with respect to their policies and consequences as an aid to lesson-learning.

The intriguing problem of the dialectic between general models and the uniqueness of nation-states is highlighted in the case of the economic crisis of the 1970s and its effect on different nation-states. True, as an economic system capitalism is an international or rather a transnational phenomenon. To speak of the 'crisis' of capitalism is to speak of a system whose field of operation is world-wide and whose problems are generic in nature (unemployment, declining profits, high interest rates, inflation and so on). Yet what is also evident is the 'uneven' nature of capitalist development and the specifics of the crisis in each *national setting*. The national context, of course, refers not simply to the economy but also to the polity – in short, to the attitudes, values and institutions within a nation-state. Both diachronic and synchronic elements are involved.

A nation has its history – economic, political, and social. At any given moment in time it also has a set of institutions through which it regulates production and distribution, manages conflict, and, more generally, makes societal decisions and maintains social values. The 'crisis' of capitalism therefore takes on a specific form as it impacts on nation-states at different points in the trajectory of their history and development. Take the United Kingdom, for example. Compared with industrial nations generally, the UK's economic performance in the post-war decades has remained sluggish. The 1960s saw a spate of books and an almost continuous debate about the state of the nation. Relatively speaking, Britain was in economic decline. In the late 1960s, joining the EEC looked like a possible way of stopping the downhill slide. But that, too, failed to cure the 'British disease'. Thus when the recession hit capitalist countries in the mid-1970s Britain already had a long history of economic decline. Continuing economic stagnation and the failure of the 'social contract' between the Labour government and trade unions ended in the 'winter of discontent'. Hyperinflation, industrial conflict and, above all, the inability to fashion an effective national consensus over crisis-management and economic recovery was the context in which the British at last turned to a radical brand of conservatism – Thatcherism.[10]

Canada provides a useful contrast. Economic growth in Canada was healthy, comparatively speaking, through the 1950s and 1960s. Inflation barely reached double-digit figures in the 1970s (see Table 3, Appendix 2). Compared with the United Kingdom, the unions and the labour movement in Canada have been and remain much weaker.[11] Not surprisingly, then, a much higher rate of unemployment has been acceptable than in Britain, thus creating a slack rather than a tight labour market. Canadian governments have found it relatively easy to order striking workers back to work and to impose statutory wage restraint.[12] Moreover, the Canadian economy managed to grow at a healthy rate through the second half of the 1970s and it was not until the early 1980s that unemployment and inflation rose into double digits and the national income showed negative growth (see Tables 1–3, Appendix 2). Clearly, the nature and severity of the economic crisis of capitalism varies from country to country depending on the political economy of the nation concerned. The nature and the course of the 'crisis' in each nation is the product of a complex interaction of a set of variables – objective and subjective – so that 'cause' and 'effect' change places readily and continuously and the process has to be seen as essentially dynamic in nature. These issues are explored later in this chapter.

In order to make sense of the economic crisis of the 1970s and various national responses to it, we have focused on a contrasting pair of policy ideologies. Needless to say, they are not value-free. Far from being merely technical devices for coping, each represents a particular value choice and favours certain group interests over others. By examining the nature of these policy models and how they have worked out in practice, we may enhance our 'lesson-learning' capabilities (what lessons we want to learn again depends in part on our class and national location). Lesson-learning, however, entails more than assessing the effectiveness of a certain approach; its feasibility is also important. Thus – to take an example from outside of the social welfare sector – the Japanese system of lifetime employment and industrial relations, although strong on effectiveness, is likely to be weak on feasibility from the viewpoint of other, especially Western, nations. Feasibility, then, refers to the possibility that the preconditions of a certain practice for a model will also be found in other nations. The question of the cultural, political and institutional prerequisites of these two models raises issues beyond the scope of this study, although we shall touch on them in the course of our explorations.[13]

## The theoretical perspective

The preceding pages have indicated in a general way the problem we intend to explore – the major policy responses to the crisis of welfare capitalism in the 1970s. Here we wish to indicate briefly the body of ideas, concepts and explanatory sketches – in short, the theory – that will be employed in the analysis. Elsewhere I have suggested an approach to the analysis of contemporary welfare states which draws chiefly upon the disciplines of sociology and political science.[14] What follows is based on that approach.

## The social system: structure and agency

It was suggested earlier that we would be looking at nation-states in our analysis of the various responses to the economic crisis of welfare capitalism. These nation-states are each seen as a social system, that is, as a configuration of institutions and groups which together form a relatively cohesive whole. This is not to take a consensus view of society. While conflict goes on, for example over distributional or normative issues, there is also cooperation through which necessary functions are performed – the production of goods and services, societal decision-making through the legislative body and so on. It is important to avoid the idea of society as either entirely conflictful or as entirely harmonious and held together by common values. Rather it is an arena of both conflict and cooperation. Moreover, the conflict versus consensus dichotomy focuses rather too much on groups and on group relationships (for example, social classes and their conflict) leaving out of account the functional or institutional sphere of society which represents the interests various groups have in common. Hence the shorthand 'national interest' is entirely legitimate. Given the present organiza- tion of peoples and economies within nation-states, each with widely varying standards of living, the nationals of a particular country may find a common cause in maintaining competitiveness, efficiency, high levels of material production and so on. If distribu- tive issues divide, productive issues tend to unite classes and groups in defence of their status as part of a nation. By and large the welfare state is based on positive-sum relations and the prospects of maintaining them.

However, society consists not only of classes and social groups but also of institutional orders. These institutional orders can be seen as forms of activity based on certain basic principles or values and organized to attain specific ends. Examples are the economic order, political order, military order, educational order, social

welfare and so on. Each of these sectors may have inbuilt
dysfunctions or contradictions which could give rise to disequilibrium and instability. The capitalist economy – privately owned,
profit-oriented and market-based – has structural imbalances in the
sense that it is only coordinated through a market mechanism,
which furthermore is subject to international influences and pressures (in this latter respect the economy is quite unlike any of the
other institutional orders). The economy is therefore prey to booms
and slumps, periodic mass unemployment and the like. The
problem here is not necessarily – indeed not primarily – one of
conflict between groups such as labour (workers) and capital
(owners) for the division of the 'pie'. Rather it is one of disequilibria
and dysfunctions arising out of the essentially pluralistic and
unplanned ('anarchic') nature of the economy. In Marxist theory
such disequilibria and disharmony are known as 'contradictions'.

Contradictions could arise *within* an institutional order (such as
the economy) or *between* different institutional orders (for example, the economy and the polity) in so far as they are based on
different social principles and might therefore be at cross-purposes.
The market economy and the democratic polity, to take two
institutional orders of capitalist society, have very different objectives and are based on very different principles. This is a potential
source of contradictions. The capitalist market economy seeks to
maximize efficiency and profit through competition. In doing so, it
rewards the efficient and punishes the inefficient. This makes the
economy a system of inequality, and an amoral one at that. It also
tends to be supranational, a feature of utmost and continuing
importance. On the other hand, the political order is firmly rooted in
the nation-state. It is based on the principle of equal participation of
citizens (each person has one vote) and 'representative' government. It may pursue objectives such as social security, equity and
environmental safety, which are of national concern. This may
require measures such as full employment, a minimum wage, a
social minimum or regulations concerning pollution and occupational health and safety – measures which run counter to the 'logic'
of a capitalist market economy. Thus, how the economy affects the
principles and values endorsed by the polity and how regulations
emanating from the polity in turn impinge on the functioning of the
economy becomes a major problem of capitalist democracies
(indeed, perhaps of all industrial societies). Harmonizing economic

and social objectives appears as a major task in all modern industrial economies.

Within the democratic polity itself there may be contradictions of one sort or another. Take, for example, the role of citizens as electors and as taxpayers. In their capacity as voters and as consumers, citizens may expect and demand a good deal from the government in the form of economic, political and social rights. At the same time, as taxpayers and as members of interest groups, they may act 'selfishly', denying government the kind of supports (willingness to pay taxes, acceptance of technical and social change, moderation in pressing wage-claims) necessary to meet their demands as voters and as consumers. Such conflicting attitudes and behaviour can also be seen as 'contradictory' in that the demands and supports within the political system do not easily equilibrate. The 'contradiction' between the welfare state (full employment and high level of social expenditure) and the capitalist market economy (which is competitive, subject to change and profit-seeking) is, of course, at the heart of the critique of welfare capitalism by both neo-conservatives and Marxists.[15] In this context the important point is that integration at the institutional or systemic and at the group or social level is, to a varying degree, interdependent. Thus institutions can work smoothly and cope with the effects of contradictions if major social groups (actors or agents) involved have 'good' relationships and are able to achieve cooperation and a measure of consensus over desired ends and the means for achieving them. Conversely, in the absence of social integration the effective functioning of institutions may be jeopardized. The problem of maintaining full employment under welfare capitalism is a good example. Success may require tripartite cooperation with respect to wage and price moderation, mobility of labour and capital, and education and training – in short the trade-off between efficiency and equity in industrial modernization.[16]

In sum, all complex social systems with some degree of system autonomy experience disequilibria of various kinds. The capitalist market economy – in its almost total reliance on market forces for regulation and in its open, supranational character – is but an extreme example of the autonomy of a system part. The idea of a social order free of contradictions is 'utopian'. That said, it also remains true that private ownership of capital and the open, international nature of the capitalist market economy make it extremely difficult to control capital as a result of the excessive autonomy of one system part. If all complex social systems are subject to contradictions, albeit differing in nature and severity, their effects can nevertheless be moderated in a variety of ways. Neo-conservative and social-corporatist approaches to harmonizing economic production and social distribution objectives are but two different ways of handling potential system contradictions of welfare capitalism. The important point, however, is that each represents a different cluster of values and a different pattern of the distribution of power and privilege in society.

### Forms of class conflict and institutional integration

We have conceptualized the social system as consisting of two levels: the level of functions and institutions and the level of interests and groups. To understand adequately the nature of the 'crisis' of welfare capitalism and the policy responses resulting from it we have to connect these two levels of analysis. The situation has to be understood as the clash of ideologies and material interests resulting from system disequilibrium.

The equilibrium represented by the post-war Keynesian welfare state, which combined economic growth with near-full employment and low inflation, came to an end in the mid-1970s. The ensuing disequilibrium was at the institutional level and was concerned primarily with the functioning of the economy. Put simply, the problem of stagflation defied solution within the Keynesian framework of economic management. This gave rise to a host of other problems such as budget deficit, rising inflation, industrial conflicts and so on. Keynesian welfare capitalism as an institutional-functional complex found itself at an impasse.

It is at such a point in the crisis of a social system that different definitions of the situation in the form of theories, ideologies and interpretations move to centre-stage. These definitions include an analysis of the nature of the crisis, its causes and possible solutions. Such theories and ideologies compete in the marketplace of ideas seeking to persuade both elites and the masses as to their 'correctness' in terms of the diagnosis and proposed remedies. In capitalist society this ideological competition and conflict can be seen largely in terms of class conflict.

But why *class*? For the simple reason that the most salient
economic division in the capitalist economy is along class lines – the
owners of capital and property, on the one hand, and the
non-propertied classes or the bulk of manual and non-manual
workers, on the other. In most capitalist democracies political
parties with their particular ideologies have also tended to be
divided roughly along class lines. In Western societies the distributional and ideological conflict between classes (broadly, the propertied and non-propertied) takes place at two different arenas: the
political and the industrial. The former refers to the electoral and
other forms of competition for policies that favour the interests of a
particular class; the latter to distributive struggles centred on
collective bargaining and industrial conflict between workers and
employers. Although highly schematic and simplified, such an
account seeks to represent the major lines of cleavage and conflict in
capitalist democracies.

Serious crises of the capitalist economy create potentials for
conflict – both ideological and material – between the major classes.
However, the relevant problems have to be defined, salient issues
raised and solutions proposed through the elaboration of ideologies. These ideologies are related to the interests of particular
groups or classes although they are invariably articulated as in the
national or general interest. Thus neo-conservatism – the ideology
espoused by the Thatcher and Reagan governments – offered a
distinctive perspective on the crisis of welfare capitalism, complete
with diagnosis and the main lines of solution. This approach
favoured strengthening the capitalist element in welfare capitalism
at the cost of the welfare element. Its prescriptions – for example,
lowering the rate of taxation on high incomes, disciplining unions,
letting unemployment find its 'natural' level (read: letting it rise) –
have favoured the interests of the owners of capital and of the
wealthy more generally. Indeed, neo-conservatism can be seen
essentially as an ideology which provides sophisticated economic
and social justification for the upward transfer of income, wealth
and power. S. M. Miller's phrase, the 'recapitalization of capitalism', sums up the change neatly provided it is taken as including the
'restratification' of capitalist society.[17] Be that as it may, the
important point is that class interests in the broader sense are at the
same time articulated as the national interest. This is clearly the case
in a democratic political order where new ideologies and new

policies based on them must be legitimized through the ballot-box. Hence the strong element of populism in the New Right's approach. The crisis of Keynesian welfare capitalism, i.e. the serious weakening of the centrist paradigm of the welfare state, created the opportunity for both the right (pro-capital interests) and the left (broadly, pro-labour interests) to define the crisis from their own perspectives and to propose new solutions. Neo-conservatism, which represents broadly the response of capital, suggested the return to a 'pure' form of capitalism – the rigour and discipline of the marketplace – including unemployment as 'natural' and inevitable in a market society, privatization, a lean even if not mean social welfare system, and reliance on non-government sectors for meeting social needs. It was a clear prescription to move to the right and away from the centrist Keynesian mixed economy of post-war capitalism.

What was the response from the left? Logically, we might have expected a parallel shift further to the extreme left in response to the crisis, i.e. a *new* 'New Left' as a radical alternative vying with the New Right for electoral support. The left's ideological options were somewhat restricted, however. The call for socialism and an end to the dominance of capital virtually meant seeking a solution outside the parameters of capitalism. For one reason or another, this has not thus far proves to be an electroally viable option. Even where the left has elaborated a programme such as the Alternative Economic Strategy, its electoral prospects have been very limited.[18] In this context the experience of the Mitterrand government is of interest.

The French Parti Socialiste formed the government in 1981 after both Thatcher and Reagan had won office. Its programme was certainly radical and initially took France in a direction which strengthened the 'welfare' aspects very considerably at the cost of 'capitalism'. However, French socialism soon retreated from this programme as economic difficulties began to mount in the context of a world recession. Within a couple of years various austerity measures were implemented in France, suggesting a retreat, which moved the country to the right in the face of the pressures of a capitalist economy.[19]

Perhaps the most successful policy response so far from the left (i.e. social democracy) has been that of *maintaining* or consolidating the welfare component of welfare capitalism. This is not so much a new ideology or even a new departure in terms of policy-making as an affirmation that Keynesian welfare capitalism could cope with the economic crisis of stagflation without sacrificing its commitment to equity or to economic efficiency and growth. It is this ability to sustain a high level of social welfare along with an efficient form of economy that distinguishes social-democratic corporatism as it is practised in Sweden and Austria.

Crises, contradictions, disequilibria and dysfunctions of a social system can up to a point be seen as 'objective' phenomena. A rising budget deficit, increasing inflation, stagnation and rising unemployment can each be regarded as an undesirable state of affairs. Moreover, if they appear in combination and persist they could pose a serious threat to economic and social well-being. But it is also clear that how problems are perceived and prioritized, which issues are seen as the 'problem' and which as 'solution', is the result of defining the situation in a particular way – in short, a matter of ideology. For example, social-democratic corporatism typically sees unemployment as an undesirable state of affairs to prevent which no stone must be left unturned, no avenue unexplored. For neo-conservatives, on the other hand, unemployment is essentially not a problem but rather a solution. It helps to lower wages, bring down inflation and promote labour discipline and mobility. Social corporatism is prepared to live with a government budget deficit – at least for some time – whereas a deficit is anathema to neo-conservative economists. A 'crisis' must therefore be seen not only as a set of objective circumstances but also as a situation which includes a subjective interpretation. In short, it is a situation which is defined in terms of ideology and group interests and which interprets the 'meaning' of economic phenomena from a particular standpoint. Indeed, we may legitimately speak of the 'social construction' of a crisis. The response to the difficulties of welfare capitalism must therefore be seen in terms of competing ideologies connected with class interests which define the situation and prepare society for change. As we have argued above, the politics of democratic capitalism is still largely a politics of class. In the vast majority of capitalist countries conservative and socialist parties have historically reflected the interest politics respectively of the propertied and non-propertied classes, broadly conceived. Organized labour, in conjunction with social-democratic or communist parties, has historically defended the interests of the non-propertied masses. It

makes sense, therefore, to speak of the *main* divide of ideology and
interests along economic class lines.

While many other forms of interest politics, based, for example,
on gender, race or religion, influence social policy, they lack the
generality and salience of class politics. Thus it is difficult to speak of
distinctive responses to the economic crisis of capitalism (i.e.
alternative strategies of managing a capitalist economy) based on
feminist or anti-racist perspectives. It is also important to bear in
mind that we are not primarily concerned with the *determinants* of
social welfare across the nations which we shall examine. Rather we
are concerned with alternative *ideologies* of welfare capitalism
which encompass the political economy of welfare and offer
credible policy alternatives. It is in this context that we speak of
capital and labour, or neo-conservatism and social democracy as
two major class-based ideologies or perspectives. However, apart
from 'class' in this sense, the perspective of social stratification also
remains important for understanding the political economy of social
welfare. Thus we shall refer to the upper, middle and lower or
working classes as broad strata representing a hierarchy of income
and occupations. Our analysis of neo-conservatism, in particular,
will emphasize distributional conflict and the differential market
capacity of social groups. Overall, the two class-related approaches
to social policy must be seen as operating within a political order
which is highly differentiated in terms of socio-economic and other
interests. It is at *this* level of analysis that gender, race, religion,
regionalism and the like assume considerable importance.

In the two chapters that follow, our focus will be on neo-conservative and social-corporatist policy models as they have worked
out in a variety of national settings. Our concern will be not so much
with the details of policies and their consequences in specific
countries as with the general experience of each country and the
nature and consequences of the policies associated with the two
models.

## Notes and references

1. See, for example, Moynihan (1969); Glazer (1971); and Kristol
   (1971). On the conception of social policy underlying the American
   War on Poverty, see Mishra (1984: 58–60).

2. Nozick (1974) is perhaps the best known work in this genre.
3. See Mishra (1984: chs 1 and 2).
4. See Mishra (1984: ch. 4), where I discuss this 'integrated welfare state' approach and contrast it with the 'differentiated welfare state' typical of post-war Britain.
5. There is a neo-Marxist as well as a neo-liberal version of this thesis. See Chapter 5, pages 102–16, for an outline and discussion of these and other interpretations of the welfare state.
6. See, for example, Krieger (1986: 5–11, 44–52).
7. On these points see Higgins (1981: ch. 2) and Jones (1985: ch. 1).
8. Briggs (1967: 33); Gilbert (1966: 231, 291–3); Lubove (1968: 4–8, 55, 56, 66–7). See also Kuhnle (1981: 126–31) for a careful appraisal of the idea of 'diffusion' of social insurance.
9. Guest (1985: ch. 8); Kitchen (1986: 33–48).
10. Krieger (1986); Gwyn and Rose (1980).
11. For example, in respect of union membership, the left vote and left governments, see Korpi (1980: 307–8); Stephens (1979: 115–18).
12. Panitch and Swartz (1985).
13. See Maier (1984) and Banting (1986) for a discussion of the preconditions of tripartism or corporatism. The present study, while not claiming to be value-free, is not intended as an exercise in policy prescription. Its main objective is to understand and interpret the nature of contemporary welfare states. The 'lesson learning' objective, in terms of alternative policies and their consequences, is meant to be of a general kind.
14. Mishra (1986).
15. See Mishra (1984: chs 2 and 3); and Gough (1979: chs 6 and 7).
16. Kuttner (1984).
17. Miller (1980: 59).
18. Conference of Socialist Economists (1980); Cripps (1981).
19. Kesselman (1986); Ross and Jenson (1983).

# 2

# The New Right: retrenching the welfare state in Britain and the United States

In this chapter we consider the extent to which the welfare state has been retrenched during the 'post-crisis' period and note the implications for equity and social justice. Our exemplars of neo-conservative social policy in action are the United States under the Reagan administration and the United Kingdom under the Thatcher government. Policies and their outcome in these two countries are examined in some detail. This is followed by a critique – based on the reasoning and evidence presented earlier in the chapter – of the thesis that the welfare state has become virtually irreversible.

The literature on the economic and social doctrine of the New Right is by now considerable.[1] We shall not attempt even an outline of its basic tenets here. Suffice to say that neo-conservatism is opposed to the key ideas and institutions of the welfare state. Put simply, the general principle behind the welfare state was that governments both could and should assume responsibility for maintaining a decent minimum standard of life for all citizens. This involved a three-pronged attack on want and dependency. First, it meant regulation of the market economy in such a way as to maintain a high and stable level of employment. Second, it meant public provision of a range of universal social services, notably education, income security, medical care and housing and an assortment of personal social services in order to meet the basic needs of citizens in a complex, changing society. Universality of social services was an important principle implying that state services were meant for all citizens and not just for the low-income population. Third, there was to be a 'safety net' of assistance services based on a test of income or means to meet exceptional cases of need and to alleviate poverty. Together these three – full employment, universal social services, and social assistance – gave concrete expression to the idea of collective responsibility for maintaining a national minimum standard of living as a matter of social right.[2] In sum, in this ideal-typical sense the welfare state institutionalized the role of the government in preventing and relieving poverty and maintaining an adequate minimum standard of life for all citizens. This implied active and ongoing intervention on the part of the nation – i.e. the government – to keep inequalities in check.[3]

The severe depression and mass unemployment of the 1930s, the breakdown of democracy and the rise of fascism, the Second World War, and the growing 'threat' of the spread of communism together formed the historical context of the post-war welfare state. The welfare state symbolized a new deal or a post-war settlement not only between capital and labour but also between capitalist democracy and its citizens in terms of certain broad guarantees and rights. These social rights of citizenship may be summed up as follows: the right to work; the right to social protection when out of work, whether temporarily or permanently; and equal access to a range of vital services, notably education and medical care, which enhanced opportunities and facilitated the individual's participation in the marketplace. Needless to say, this represents an ideal-type of the welfare state to which some countries approximated more closely than others.[4]

Following the OPEC price shock of 1973 and the onset of stagflation in the mid-1970s, Western governments generally found it increasingly difficult to maintain a commitment to the welfare state. The goal of full employment was first to be abandoned by many governments, while restraint on social expenditure became commonplace.[5] However, what distinguished the New Right from other more pragmatic responses was its rejection of the welfare state *in principle*. This rejection implied that the objectives and methods of the welfare state were incompatible with economic progress in a capitalist society. Rolling back the frontier of social welfare was therefore necessary to enable the market economy and free society to survive. Predecessors of neo-conservative regimes –

the Carter administration in the United States and the Callaghan government in the United Kingdom – had already embarked upon measures such as allowing unemployment to rise and reducing social expenditure, which made subsequent neo-conservative policies in these countries seem more a matter of degree than of kind.[6] It would be a mistake, however, to overlook the important difference between the Reagan and Thatcher regimes, on the one hand, and their predecessors, on the other. True, both Carter and Callaghan administrations failed to defend the welfare state. But neo-conservative governments introduced a qualitatively new dimension to the picture. The basic objectives and methods of the welfare state were to be abandoned in favour of a new type of social order, the construction of which became the project of the New Right.

## Farewell to full employment

During the 1950s and 1960s unemployment in Britain stood between 1% and 2%. It began to rise in the 1970s, seesawing between 4% and 6% by the late 1970s (see Table 1, Appendix 2).[7] The Labour government's historic accord with trade unions, which was intended to reduce unemployment, contain inflation and reflate the economy, broke down in the winter of 1978–9. Its consequence was the electoral success of conservatives under Thatcher's leadership.

The Thatcher government came to power on a broad neo-conservative platform. According to this ideology, governments could not maintain full employment without creating adverse effects such as inflation and declining productivity. The lesson was that governments should not try to maintain employment 'artificially' but rather allow market forces to determine 'natural' employment levels. Moreover, the monetarist approach for dealing with inflation meant a squeeze on the economy (deflation) with the understanding that this was bound to increase unemployment. Unemployment therefore essentially became part of the solution rather than the problem, at least in the short run.

The Thatcher government's deflationary policy coincided with a world recession and sent unemployment soaring. From around 1.3

million in 1979 it rose to more than 2.5 million in 1981, doubling the unemployment rate from 4.5% to 9.1%. Thereafter the relentless climb of unemployment continued as Britain remained in the grip of a hardline monetarist policy. By early 1985, over 3 million were unemployed by official counts, while unofficial estimates put the figure at 4 million, or 13% of the labour force.[8] Clearly, neo-conservatism had dispensed with the idea that governments could or should be held responsible for maintaining employment. The Thatcher government has repeatedly affirmed that its main priority was controlling and reducing inflation. As for creating jobs, it was largely up to employers (enterprise and investment) and workers themselves to increase productivity and to price themselves into jobs.[9]

In the United States full employment had never been accepted as a government responsibility.[10] In the 1950s and 1960s unemployment averaged between 4% and 5%. It rose during the 1970s and stood at 7.6% when Reagan assumed office in 1981.[11] Like Thatcherism, Reaganomics put its trust in market forces to create jobs and to determine the level of employment. It also relied on a monetarist deflationary policy as the means to control inflation. By 1982 the combination of monetarism and high interest rates set off a recession which pushed unemployment up to 9.7%. Unlike the United Kingdom, however, the United States managed to produce a strong economic recovery in 1983–4 which brought unemployment down. By 1986 the unemployment rate had returned to the level of the late 1970s.[12]

In retrospect it is clear that the government's success in returning unemployment to at least pre-Reagan levels had little to do with monetarism, market forces or other neo-conservative nostrums. It owed more to the boost provided by a huge increase in military spending financed through the largest budget deficit in American history.[13] Taxes on the rich and on corporations were also substantially reduced, ostensibly following the precepts of supply-side economics. As a result the budget deficit, which was only 1.0% of gross domestic product (GDP) in 1981 rose to 3.8% in 1983. In 1986 it was still 3.5% (see Table 4, Appendix 2).[14] Clearly the economic recovery and the improvement in the job situation owed a great deal to the policy of military Keynesianism – tax reduction and the deficit financing of military expenditure by the government. The United Kingdom, which played the monetarist game more faithfully, has had far less success with respect to economic growth and unemployment.[15]

According to neo-conservatives unemployment is unavoidable in market economies. It is the price to be paid for freedom of enterprise and growth. But how do neo-conservative regimes treat the unemployed? How are those who are chosen to pay the price for economic progress treated with respect to income security and living standards? Starting from very different bases of unemployment compensation, both countries have made sizeable cuts in benefits. In Britain earnings-related supplements to basic flat-rate insurance benefits were reduced in 1981 and then abolished in 1982. In that year benefits also became taxable.[16] With the rise in long-term unemployment the unemployed and their dependents have had to resort to means-tested social security benefits in increasing numbers.[17]

In the United States Congress restrained the administration's hands with respect to cutbacks on unemployment compensation. Even so, extended benefits for the unemployed were reduced and the supplemental benefits which were approved were less generous than in previous recessions. Federal cutbacks had a knock-on effect on the states, which determine eligibility and benefit levels above a federally mandated minimum. As a result of these restrictions only 45% of the unemployed received benefits during the recession of 1982 compared with 75% in 1975, the previous peak period of recession.[18] By the end of 1984 coverage had dropped to about 25% of the unemployed, the lowest on record since unemployment insurance began.[19]

In the United Kingdom unemployment benefits are nationally standardized. Moreover, Britons are entitled to *nationally administered* social assistance benefits, subject to a means test. By contrast, American unemployed workers are at the mercy of the states. Both eligibility and benefit levels vary a good deal from one state to another. In most states single persons and families without children under age 18 are not eligible for cash public assistance, though some may be eligible for food stamps.[20] Unemployment often means that workers and their dependents lose the health insurance coverage (provided by the employers) together with their jobs, as there is no medical care programme in the United States for the general population. Moreover, the unemployed often find themselves ineligible for Medicaid, the means-tested programme of medical assistance.[21]

## Universal social services

A range of universal services aimed at meeting the basic needs of the population in a modern industrial society constitutes perhaps the core element of the post-war welfare state. Significantly enough, universal services have suffered only minor impairments in both the United Kingdom and the United States. Although neo-conservatives are opposed in principle to universality and would prefer a selective approach, in practice they have not been able to retrench universal services such as medical care, old-age pensions and education. The major reason for this would seem to be the widespread and continuing popular support for these services.[22] Since they are enjoyed by all or the vast majority of income classes and social groups, the constituency for them is nation-wide. Not surprisingly, both Reagan and Thatcher regimes backed away from direct proposals to retrench or privatize them.

In the United Kingdom the Central Policy Review Staff (the government's 'think tank') proposed sweeping changes in education, social security and health services in September 1982. These proposals included the deindexing of social security benefits, replacing the NHS with a private health insurance scheme and the ending of state financing of institutions of higher education. The widespread outcry provoked by this confidential document (which was leaked) and the pressures of an election year led to a series of statements from the government ruling out such radical measures, including Thatcher's assurance that the National Health Service was 'safe with us'.[23] Proposals along somewhat similar lines have continued to emanate from right-wing policy institutes from time to time but have not been considered politically feasible.

Housing is one area, however, where there has been a very considerable retrenchment of public provision in Britain. Council (municipal) housing, which in the main serves manual workers and other relatively low-income households, has suffered a major cutback. Public housing completions, which had been reduced from more than 160,000 in the mid-1970s to 104,000 in 1979, fell below 50,000 in 1982, the lowest level in fifty years. By 1986 completions were down to around 30,000. During 1979–82 council rents more than doubled as subsidies were cut drastically. However, low-income tenants became eligible for housing assistance, an item of government expenditure that has risen substantially. Undoubtedly housing is one area in which the government has pursued its objectives of privatization with considerable *élan*. Over 1 million council houses (about 15% of existing stock) have been sold to sitting tenants at an average discount of 44% of their market valuation.[24]

Apart from the changes in unemployment insurance benefits noted above, the transfer of the sickness benefit scheme in 1983 from national insurance to employers and the cut in benefits under the State Earnings-Related Pension Scheme (the government is encouraging private or occupational pension supplements instead) are among the notable changes in income security in Britain.[25] The government has tried to promote the growth of private health insurance in a variety of ways. It has also increased user charges substantially and sought to privatize ancillary services (such as catering and laundry) within the National Health Service. There is considerable evidence to suggest that the government is holding down expenditure on health services as a means of stimulating the growth of private medicine.[26] On the other hand, the expectation that private health insurance would cover about a quarter of the population by the mid-1980s has proved wide of the mark. Private health insurance coverage rose from 3.9% of the population in 1976 to 8.0% in 1986. Under present circumstances it seems unlikely that it will expand further.[27] The mainstay of the New Right's approach in privatizing education has been the introduction of a system of vouchers. For both political and financial reasons, however, it has not proved feasible.

In sum, the main universal services – income maintenance, health care and education (although not housing) – can be said to have survived eight years of neo-conservative rule in Britain with only relatively minor impairments. The level of expenditure on these services also shows no evidence of *serious* underfunding. We shall return to the question of the long-term erosion of these services through underfunding and increasing privatization and also through certain other changes in government policy, notably taxation.

In the United States universal services are a good deal less developed than they are in the United Kingdom. There is no general health insurance for the population, only an insurance programme for those over 65 (Medicare). Income maintenance programmes such as sickness and maternity benefits (temporary disability) and family allowances, which are commonplace in most industrialized nations, have not been instituted in the United States. Not surprisingly, means-tested services account for a sizeable proportion of social expenditure. In the early 1980s for instance, more than 20% of social expenditure in the United States was on means-tested benefits, compared with less than 1% in Sweden.[28] Indeed, the 1970s saw a rise in this percentage as the war on poverty led to the expansion of means-tested benefits such as Medicaid, food stamps and general welfare (Aid to Families with Dependent Children (AFDC)).[29]

Ideological and political support for the welfare state has been a good deal weaker in the United States than in the United Kingdom. Not surprisingly, the Reagan platform included plans for substantial cuts in social services and expenditures, whereas the pronouncements of British Conservatives on social policy and expenditure have been couched in more general terms about encouraging private initiatives and reducing government involvement.[30] In any case universal services in both countries have escaped largely unscathed. The Reagan administration had planned much smaller reductions in these compared with reductions in means-tested programmes, although it is the former that are far more expensive, and ended up with even smaller reductions than what it wanted.[31] The administration's proposal of May 1981 sought to reduce early retirement benefits, restrict eligibility for disabled persons and prevent benefit levels from rising as rapidly as wage levels. The proposal was rejected unanimously by Congress.[32] Among universal income maintenance programmes only unemployment insurance has suffered substantial reduction (see page 22 above). It is scarcely a coincidence that compared with old-age pensions, a social insurance programme which benefits the entire insured population, unemployment insurance has a far smaller effective benefit population.

As in the United Kingdom, right-wing think tanks in the United States have also made radical proposals for the privatization of pensions and medical care services. These include the Family Security Plan developed by the Heritage Foundation, which would replace social security with an Individual Retirement Account and allow social security taxes to go towards the purchase of private pensions. Similar proposals have been made for Individual Health Accounts.[33] The use of vouchers in the provision of education and other services has also been widely touted but with little practical impact so far. As in the case of Britain, prospects for the erosion of universal social services in light of other policies of neo-conservatives, notably in respect of taxation and the budget deficit, must be reserved for discussion later. For the moment we must conclude that social security, education and medicare have suffered only minor impairments *so far*.

## Poverty and basic minimum standards

To a large extent full employment and a range of universal services to meet basic needs together constitute the major defence against poverty in the welfare state and the first line of defence for a national minimum standard of living. In addition, a specific commitment towards protecting the living standards of the low-income and other vulnerable groups constitutes the second line of defence. This might involve measures such as a minimum wage, income supplementation, job creation, and education and training. As we have seen, neo-conservatives have abandoned full employment as a goal of social policy and weakened universal services, without, however, being able to retrench them. As regards the third component of the welfare state – the social safety net for low-income and other vulnerable households – that has been virtually abandoned by neo-conservatives in principle and weakened a good deal in practice. It is the low-income and other vulnerable minority groups who have had to bear the brunt of the social policy of the New Right. This is the reality, notwithstanding conservative rhetoric about selectivity and maintaining the safety net for the truly needy.

In Britain, as we have seen, council housing, which benefits manual workers and other low-income households, has suffered major cutbacks. While means-tested housing allowances have to some extent cushioned the impact of the increase in council housing rents, many households have suffered a sharp decline in living standards as a result of higher rents.[34] The long-term effects of privatization on the supply of affordable housing remain somewhat speculative. The immediate effects are clearer. The Thatcher government's pro-capital and pro-market policies have affected the housing situation of the low-income population quite adversely. In recent years house prices have risen dramatically, making it virtually impossible for first-time buyers (the young and other low- to middle-income groups) to secure a foothold in the housing market. Overall, the impact of government policy, seen in conjunction with high unemployment, has been to increase dramatically the number of homeless.[35]

Rather than protecting low-wage and non-unionized workers, the Thatcher government has favoured deregulation. Thus the wages councils which regulated minimum wages for about 3 million workers have been weakened very substantially.[36] At the moment, therefore, low-paid workers in Britain are without the protection of either a statutory minimum wage or wages councils. Unemployment, the weakening of union power and deregulation of low wages have all had their impact on wage levels. The proportion of low-paid workers in Britain increased from 36% in 1979 to 41% in 1985.[37] During the 1980s the Thatcher government also increased user charges especially in the health sector (for example, medical prescriptions and dental services). These bear heavily on the low-income population and act as a deterrent even where means-tested assistance is available.[38] More recent changes under the Social Security Act of 1986 (effective April 1988) have made the situation of the low-income population still worse.[39]

As a result of unemployment, the growth of low-wage jobs, higher social service charges and other government policies (notably regressive taxation, discussed below) the population living in poverty increased markedly after 1979 to 7.2 million or 13.5% of the total population in 1983.[40] In 1985 the population in poverty was officially estimated at 9.4 million, a 55% increase since 1979. For the 1979–87 period the Low Pay Unit estimates the increase to have been 85%.[41] If the Thatcher government has had some political commitment towards maintaining mainstream services such as education and health care it has no such commitment, and certainly no ideological commitment, to maintaining the living standards of the poor.

For the New Right poverty represents an absolute rather than a relative concept. There is therefore no 'legitimate agenda for collective choice beyond the issue of absolute poverty'.[42] This approach harks back to restricting the role of the state to the relief of *destitution* rather than to the relief of poverty and relying on the generosity of the rich and fortunate to help their unfortunate fellows, as was the case in Victorian Britain.[43] Following the classical notions of individualism and the superiority of the market principle elaborated by such thinkers as Herbert Spencer and Friedrich von Hayek, this ideology proclaims relative poverty and inequality as desirable by-products of freedom and the rule of the marketplace.

In the United States cutbacks in social services and expenditures have been far deeper and more extensive than in the United Kingdom. On the other hand, unemployment is a good deal lower and mitigates somewhat the effects of cutbacks on living standards. Unlike the Thatcher government, with its indirect approach to reducing social welfare programmes, the Reagan administration was more open and upfront in its plans to retrench social programmes and expenditures. President Reagan's initial proposals envisaged an overall reduction of 17% in social spending compared with the plans of the Carter administration. In the event the reduction was of the order of 10%, with low-income programmes bearing the brunt of the reduction.[44] Thus despite Reagan's rhetoric about the safety net and protecting the poor, cutbacks in programmes such as general welfare (AFDC) and food stamps were substantial. For example, through tighter eligibility rules nearly half a million families were eliminated from AFDC rolls, almost all of them low-income families headed by women, while more than a quarter of a million had their benefits reduced.[45] Medical assistance (Medicaid) was also cut. Since eligibility for Medicaid is linked to AFDC, most of those displaced from AFDC also lost their medical benefits.[46] More than 1 million people lost their eligibility for food stamps, while the rest had their benefit levels reduced.[47] Overall, the greatest losers through these changes were the working poor. Since women and children are heavily represented among low-income individuals, they have suffered disproportionately. It is estimated that nearly one-third of all children now living in poverty in the United States are without medical assistance because their families have lost eligibility for Medicaid.[48]

If the United States has a lower rate of unemployment it nevertheless leads the United Kingdom in the proliferation of low-wage jobs. Most of the jobs lost were unionized and highly paid, for example in the automobile, steel and other goods-producing sectors. New jobs are mainly in the low-paying service sector such as retail trade, hotel and motel and hospital sectors.[49] At $9,000 a year, the average wage in retailing is less than half the average wage in manufacturing.[50] As a result, real wages are now lower than at any time during the 1970s. According to one 1987 study, more than half the jobs created since 1980 paid less than the poverty-level income for a family of four.[51] In 1984 close to 8 million workers received wages at or below the minimum wage of $3.35 an hour; this minimum wage had not been raised since the Carter administration.[52] The Reagan administration's strong anti-union policy also helped reduce wages and other forms of compensation for workers. Moreover, cutbacks in unemployment and disability benefits are designed to induce Americans to accept and to hold low-wage jobs. Clearly Thatcher conservatives would like to see the United Kingdom move in this direction.

The cumulative effect of high unemployment down to the mid-1980s, the decline in wages and cutbacks in social programmes can be seen in the rise of poverty population in the United States. Poverty, which declined from 12.6% in 1970 to 11.7% in 1979, began to rise again in 1980, reaching a new peak of 15.2% in 1983. It came down following the economic recovery but in 1985 still stood at 14%, or more than two percentage points higher than in 1979. Some 33 million people remained in poverty, 7 million more than in 1979.[53] Moreover, the poverty gap has widened by as much as 50% since 1977, leaving those below the poverty line much worse off than before.[54]

Although taxation policy has only an indirect bearing on issues of the welfare state it is far too important to be left out of account. For one, public, including social, expenditure has to be financed largely out of taxation. For another, the nature and level of taxation have major implications for inequality and income redistribution.

Neo-conservative regimes are opposed to 'confiscation' – public levy on the income of individuals or firms generated through the market. It is argued that such taxation amounts to an encroachment on property rights and acts as a disincentive to enterprise and wealth creation. The so-called 'supply-side' economics of the New Right has elaborated these beliefs into a series of theoretical propositions. These entail wild claims about the miraculous effect of tax reduction on economic growth, producing higher revenues for the government at lower levels of taxation. At any rate both Thatcher and Reagan governments came to power on the pledge to reduce taxes, especially taxes on personal income and on business. In the United Kingdom these taxes have been lowered gradually in keeping with the monetarist philosophy of public finance (i.e. without an increase in the budget deficit). In the United States, however, supply-side considerations were more prominent. The Reagan administration therefore implemented huge tax cuts from the outset apparently on the assumption that this would lead to a great surge of economic activity which would in turn produce higher revenues and reduce the deficit.

In the United Kingdom the first Thatcher government lowered the top marginal rate of tax on earned income from 83% to 60% and cut the basic rate of income tax from 33% to 30%. There were other, somewhat minor, reductions in investment income and capital taxes. On the other hand, in part to finance these cuts, indirect taxation (notably the value-added tax) was raised. In short, progressive taxes were reduced and regressive taxes increased, a policy that has continued throughout the three Thatcher governments at varying pace and intervals.[55] Whereas higher-income groups have continued to receive tax breaks, lower- and middle-income groups have found their tax burden increased through indirect taxation and higher social security taxes.[56] In addition, many charges and fees have been increased, especially in the National Health Service.[57]

In 1984 an estimated £4.17 billion was lost in tax revenues through changes introduced since 1979 by the Thatcher government. Forty-four per cent of this tax handout went to the top 1% of taxpayers, while a mere 3% went to the bottom 25% of taxpayers.[58] Following the deflationary policy and the resulting recession of the early 1980s, the British economy made a gradual recovery. More recently there has been steady, if moderate, growth, slightly higher than the average for OECD countries (see Table 2, Appendix 2). However, instead of channelling some of this growth into the social services, which were badly in need of funds, the government decided to use it to finance further tax cuts. Indeed, the government's budget of March 1988 established a new top marginal tax rate of 40%, sweeping away higher income-tax rates of between 45% and 60%. The new rate is apparently the lowest top tax rate of any leading market economy. The standard rate of income tax has also been lowered slightly. Of the total tax cut of £6 billion, one-third went to the top 5% of taxpayers.[59] According to a leading English weekly, these changes represent 'the final disappearance of the last vestiges of the post-war consensus'. The idea of fairness and justice as expressed through the tax system is no longer even 'the pretended aspiration of the Conservative Party'.[60] This is supply-side Reaganomics with a vengeance. Stripped of rationalization and rhetoric, the government's tax policies are part and parcel of a major programme of upward redistribution of income.

In the United States the first major tax cuts came in the first presidential budget of 1981, which reduced the top rate of tax on unearned income from 70% to 50% and the maximum rate on capital gains from 28% to 20%. There was also an across-the-board reduction in income-tax rates for all taxpayers spread over three years, a reduction which gave high-income groups proportionately more in tax relief.[61] As Palmer and Sawhill write: 'Unlike the program cuts, which served mainly to reduce the incomes of poorer families, personal income and tax cuts served mainly to raise the after-tax incomes of more affluent families.'[62] Other tax cuts, notably those for businesses, liberalized treatment of Individual Retirement Accounts, and reductions in gift and inheritance taxes have reinforced the inequality of treatment.[63] The combined effect of social spending cuts, other budget changes and the large, regressive changes in taxation has produced a huge upward redistribution of income in the United States. It is estimated that over the 1983–5 period households making less than $20,000 a year lost $20 billion in income, whereas those making more than $80,000 gained $35 billion. Those at the bottom of the income distribution (with incomes less than $10,000 a year) lost an average of $1,100 a year over 1983–5; those at the top (with incomes of $200,000 or more) made an average gain of $60,000 a year.[64]

A dramatic and long-term consequence of the Reagan tax cuts, coupled with a sharp increase in military spending, was to increase the budget deficit enormously. In the twelve months from 1981 to 1982 the federal deficit almost doubled from $58 billion to $111 billion, and over the next three years almost quadrupled, rising to $212 billion in 1985. This represented an increase from 2% to 5.4% of gross national product (GNP).[65] On the other hand, government revenues fell from 21.1% of GNP in 1981 to 18.6% in 1985.[66] One result of the large deficit created by the Reagan administration was the passage of the Gramm–Rudman–Hollings Act (December 1985) which mandates automatic cuts annually, culminating in a balanced budget in 1991.[67] The implications for social expenditures of the reduction in taxes and the Gramm–Rudman–Hollings Act are considered below.

## The 'irreversible' welfare state or the new 'two-nation' state?

The previous section has attempted an outline of recent develop-ments in neo-conservative regimes in relation to the three com-ponents of the welfare state. As we have seen, full employment has been abandoned as public policy, while programmes serving the low-income population have suffered disproportionately from cutbacks. On the other hand, universal social programmes remain largely intact. Moreover, even low-income services have in the main suffered erosion and cutbacks rather than outright abolition. The aggregate level of social spending in these countries has changed little.

How, then, do we assess the success of neo-conservatism in charting a new course? Has the New Right failed in its attack on the welfare state? Indeed, was there an 'attack' at all? Has the new ideology turned out to be 'full of sound and fury, signifying nothing'? Moreover, if such an ideologically intransigent assault on the welfare state as represented by the Thatcher and Reagan regimes has failed, then what prospect do other countries have of achieving similar objectives? These are important questions which demand a satisfactory answer.

There is by now a sizeable literature on the implications of the New Right for the welfare state. In this literature the question whether the project of rolling back the welfare state has succeeded has been answered largely in the negative. Perhaps this line of thought is best summed up by the idea that, given the continuation of a liberal electoral democracy, the welfare state becomes 'irre-versible'. With only minor differences, social scientists of varying theoretical persuasion such as Offe, Therborn, Piven and Cloward, LeGrand and O'Higgins concur that the reality in these two countries is very different from the rhetoric of the New Right.[68] Thus apropos of the first five years of Thatcher government,

LeGrand and Winter ask why, 'despite facing the most serious ideological assault it had encountered since its inception', the welfare state has proved 'so remarkably resilient'. They go on to observe that,

far from being reduced, during the first five years of the new administration public expenditure increased in real terms in most areas of welfare provision; moreover, with the important exception of the sale of council houses, other forms of privatization were minimal.[69]

On the other side of the Atlantic Piven and Cloward concede somewhat greater success to the Reagan regime. But they, too, find that Offe's summing up of the situation in Europe is valid for the United States – that 'widespread enthusiasm for the strategy of abolishing the welfare state and tightening other peoples' belts has not been translated into results of more than a marginal scope'.[70] Piven and Cloward agree that in the United States, as in Britain and elsewhere in Western Europe, the welfare state had 'shown a remarkable durability'.[71] Ruggles and O'Higgins, after examining the retrenchment of social welfare in Britain and the United States down to the mid-1980s, conclude:

while Reagan and Thatcher began with visions of major structural rollbacks and remarketization of welfare provision – visions whose failure could easily be foreseen – they have moved to an acceptance of the structural role of welfare in democratic mixed economies and are now focussing on ways of constraining and redistributing its cost.[72]

Any consideration of the major retrenchment or reversibility of the welfare state raises the question of how we define the 'welfare state'. In the literature referred to above, attention has naturally enough been focused, first, on the aggregate level of social expenditure, and second, on the entitlement of benefits and services under mainstream programmes of income security, medical care and education. Sometimes, however, a very specific definition has been chosen. For example, Therborn defines it in terms of the major activities of the state. Thus, he writes, 'it was in the 1970s that most advanced capitalist states became welfare states, in the sense that welfare expenditure became the predominant kind of state spending'.[73]

It is arguable that while social expenditures and mainstream programmes are the most visible aspects of the welfare state, an

exclusive focus on these runs the risk of leaving out of account
certain other significant changes that have taken place. In this book
we have defined the welfare state more in sociological terms and less
in terms of public finance and the current size of the public sector in
welfare. Although quantitative indicators are necessary and
important, care must be taken not to fall into the positivist trap and
lose sight of the different 'meanings' that nominally identical data
embody. To take an obvious example: contrary to the Thatcher
government's intention, public expenditure, far from being reduced, in fact grew from 39.5% of GDP in 1979–80 to 42.0% in
1980–1 and to 43.5% in 1981–2. At the end of the first Thatcher
government it stood at 42.5% of GDP or three full percentage
points higher than when the government took office. Moreover, in
real terms *social* expenditure rose by about 10% during the same
period.[74] A superficial reading of these figures suggests an *expansion* rather than *contraction* of the welfare state. However, a
somewhat different reading of the situation emerges when the
major role of unemployment benefits in boosting state expenditure
is recognized. Undoubtedly, from a public finance and budgetary
viewpoint, the British welfare state may be said to have *grown*
rather than *shrunk* during these years. But if one takes a sociological and political view of the welfare state then such a conclusion
would be entirely unwarranted. It is important to define social
welfare in *meaningful* terms, failing which the use of expenditure
data as a proxy for the welfare state could easily lead us astray.

Let us recapitulate the definition of the welfare state used in this
book. It is the institutionalization of government responsibility for
maintaining national minimum standards. In the post-war welfare
state this meant primarily three types of commitment and institutions: policies of full employment, universal services for meeting
basic needs, and a variety of measures for preventing and relieving
poverty. We have sought to demonstrate that the New Right has
been successful in deinstitutionalizing the welfare state in two of
these three aspects: in rejecting government responsibility for
maintaining high levels of employment; and in repudiating, in
practice if not in principle, government responsibility for preventing poverty and for maintaining minimum standards. True, large-
scale unemployment now coexists with all kinds of political regime
and in this sense has little to do with New Right policy. But in so far
as that is the case, then those regimes also have effectively

abandoned an important tenet of the welfare state. It is neo-conservatism, however, that has made monetarism, deflation and the recommodification of labour as part of its credo. From this perspective unemployment appears as a natural concomitant of a market economy. The retreat from a policy of a national minimum is most evident in the targeting of cutbacks on the low-income population, especially prominent in the United States; the abolition of wages councils in Britain; stricter eligibility and lower benefits for social security recipients such as the unemployed and the homeless; and, above all, in grossly inequitable taxation policies in which the departure from the assumptions and practices of the era of the welfare state is most evident. True, if the focus is on social services and programmes alone, then even cutbacks affecting the poor may be said to have been modest, especially in the United Kingdom. At any rate this would appear to be the case if the situation is seen from a broad institutional viewpoint rather than from a distributional and stratification perspective, including individual life chances. But, not surprisingly, the increase in poverty in both the United Kingdom and the United States, despite the economic boom in the latter – as measured by the proportion of poverty population, the growth in the poverty gap in low-wage occupations and in the numbers of the working poor – indicates a major change with respect to inequality which cannot be captured by social expenditure statistics.

Even with respect to the 'core' element of the welfare state – mainstream universal services – the situation may not be quite as 'irreversible' as suggested by a look at current programmes and expenditures. No doubt it is these heartland services – education, medical care and pensions – that receive the strongest support from the public and it is in their attempt to retrench this major area of social welfare spending that New Right regimes have had the least success. However, as Taylor-Gooby, for example, has shown, public support for these state services is not unequivocal. Proposals for privatization also command a good deal of support, suggesting an instrumental approach on the part of citizens.[75] It is precisely in this context that selective privatization, the approach of the Thatcher government, for example, may become an important instrument for weakening the universalist structure of these services and for paving the way to their residualization. In the area of income support services, for example pensions, the move away from public and towards private provision is already well advanced.

Public housing, which stands half-way between a universal and a low-income service, is being privatized on a large scale. In the case of education and health care, too, if standards decline through underfunding and if private alternatives are made available through further concessions, then the universalist nature of these services could conceivably begin to crumble. As Taylor-Gooby writes:

> Exit, for most people, is an impossibly expensive option. However, if voice fails and standards do not improve, and if government widens opportunities for exit from direct state provision, loyalty to the mass services may be speedily undermined. This is the effect of the subsidies of the 1986 Act, the discounts for home ownership under the 'right to buy' scheme and the provision for transferring from state to quasi-private schooling in the 1987 Education Bill.[76]

It is not unlikely that just as 'retrenchment in direct provision for unfavoured groups, such as the unemployed, has generated little opposition, the expansion of private welfare services may pave the way to further contraction in welfare provision without public opinion backlash'.[77] In short, we cannot consider the issue of 'reversibility' settled. The same logic which has enabled neo-conservatives in the United States and to a lesser extent in the United Kingdom to cut benefits and programmes for less favoured minorities could enable these regimes to differentiate further up the stratification scale. Given vested interests and electoral politics, a sudden and dramatic dismantling of these services was perhaps never a realistic option for neo-conservative governments. On the other hand, as the Thatcher administration, for example, has shown, these governments are capable of sustaining a long-term commitment to radical change. It would be too soon to pronounce them paper tigers as far as the retrenchment of mainstream services is concerned.

In this connection it is useful to distinguish between a number of different, if overlapping, issues: the *ideology* and/or the political *rhetoric* of the New Right; its party political *platform* in respect of social policy; the policy *agenda* and its *implementation* by neo-conservative governments; and the actual *outcome* and extent of change. Most observers have focused attention on the first and last of these issues and, not surprisingly, found a yawning gap between them. Clearly no radical government, whether of the left or the right, working within parliamentary and institutional constraints, can be expected to shape economic and social policy according to the dictates of ideology. In this sense a gap between rhetoric and reality is inevitable. Moreover, if we look at the electoral programmes and other specific policy statements of neo-conservatives, we cannot say that retrenching the welfare state has been one of their features. This is clear at least in the case of the Thatcher government through all three terms of office. Analysis therefore runs the risk of being both inadequate and seriously misleading if it contrasts New Right ideology and rhetoric, which no doubt suggests a return to a residual social policy, with actual policy consequences – without examining the intervening variables of party programme and government agenda in respect of social policy. A more appropriate comparison would be between rhetoric and ideology with extremely *radical* connotations, on the one hand, and a cautious electoral platform and policy implementation, on the other. Equally relevant would be a comparison between policy objectives and *expected* outcomes, on the one hand, and *actual* outcomes, on the other. But to juxtapose the heady rhetoric and sweeping prescriptions of the ideologues of the New Right with the small coinage of real change is to deflect attention away from the very real changes that have taken place and from those that are being brought about in a piecemeal fashion. It is also to lose sight of the *process* that is involved, that is, the very important steps which connect ideology with political practice.

In a paper published well before the March 1988 budget of the Thatcher government, Ruggles and O'Higgins pointed to the quite radical changes achieved by the new right in certain policy areas, such as taxation. These changes are not without relevance to the question of the retrenchment of the welfare state. As Ruggles and O'Higgins remark, the new tax policies 'leave lower-income groups paying a larger share of any tax-financed increases in government spending' which both generates extra resistance to spending and provides the government with additional reasons for not spending.[78] Cost containment and the decline of the quality of public service may be expected to lead to more private alternatives especially in times of increasing private prosperity. In other words, universality may be weakened by attrition rather than by assault. The March 1988 tax cuts in Britain (see pages 30–1 above) provide a striking illustration of the attrition strategy. Economic growth, combined with the sale of public assets, has helped generate a budget surplus in place of the usual deficit. However, rather than allocate much-needed funds to medicare or other social services, the government has chosen to give away massive tax cuts to the rich. As mentioned earlier, in the United States the Gramm–Rudman–Hollings Act provides for automatic annual budget cuts, culminating in a balanced budget in 1991. Under the Act Congress has begun budget cuts, although for the moment social security and some of the programmes affecting the poor have been spared. But as Palmer and Sawhill point out, the large deficit bequeathed by the Reagan administration is an important means of applying a brake to social spending.[79] Whether or not universal social programmes are irreversible may in the long run depend on whether tax cuts implemented by Reagan and Thatcher prove reversible.

In sum, the changes wrought by the New Right in the United States and in the United Kingdom with respect to the values and institutions represented by the welfare state cannot be understood in terms of a simple dichotomy such as the reversibility/irreversibility of the welfare state. First, the thesis of irreversibility focuses somewhat narrowly on universal social programmes or, worse, on aggregate social expenditures, ignoring important reversals with respect to full employment, entitlement to a basic minimum and protection from poverty. Second, the irreversibility thesis seems to ignore the implications of a host of changes brought about or set in motion by the New Right for the possible erosion of the heartland services of the welfare state. Indeed, the consequences of the partial retrenchment of the welfare state take on added significance when seen in the context of certain other changes taking place in all advanced industrial economies.

It is well known, for instance, that in advanced industrial, especially capitalist, countries the mass production of goods is requiring less and less labour. New high-technology industries are developing which are often small-scale and employ relatively few workers. The main area of occupational growth appears to be the service sector. In the literature of political economy this change is sometimes expressed as the transition from the Fordist (that is, mass production of goods with a large army of blue-collar workers) to the post-Fordist form of production. In the context of a market economy the latter tends to generate an occupational pattern polarized into a relatively small, highly skilled and well-paid sector and a relatively large, low-skilled and low-paid sector. This transition to post-Fordism through the market economy involves the decline of relatively well-paid skilled manual jobs typical of the automobile or steel industry and the growth of a large number of low-skilled and low-paid jobs in services and also in the new electronics and computer industries.[80] A good deal of the social policy of the New Right in the United States and in Britain can be seen as facilitating this transition. For instance, the acceptance of unemployment as a necessary price for the restructuring of industry and capital, the reduction in unemployment benefits and coverage, the emasculation of trade unions, the demand that workers 'price themselves into jobs' (read: accept low wages), deregulation of the labour market, for example through the abolition of wages councils in Britain, together with the growth of part-time employment of women benefit employers by enabling marginal workers to be hired at low wages and without fringe benefits. They also discourage labour unions and thus promote a more 'flexible' workforce.

The transition to a post-Fordist form of production and concomitant labour-market changes tend to create a 'dual economy' in the sense of a polarized occupational and wage structure. The New Right's social policy can be seen as helping to restructure the labour market along these lines and furthering the development of a dual economy and society. This new tendency towards the development of a 'two-nation society', especially in countries dominated by the New Right, has already been noted. Ideal-typically the division seems to be between a 'core' and a 'periphery'. As taxes are increasingly lowered and as public services are allowed to deteriorate, those belonging to the core – the population with full-time jobs, good incomes and work-related benefits – will have the prospect of buying services in the private market. The periphery would consist of a minority of the working and non-working poor who must rely on increasingly marginalized and ghettoized public services. Such poor are sure to include socially disadvantaged groups such as ethnic minorities, female-headed households, the long-term unemployed, the homeless, and the aged and disabled without occupational pensions.

More recently, some irreversibility theorists have come to recognize these developments and their significance for the reversal of the welfare state. The long-term objectives of the New Right's social policy and its continuity along these lines are gradually being acknowledged. Thus, according to Therborn, 'consciously or unconsciously', the development of a 'dualistic economy and society – a dynamic well-off sector and a stagnating or declining sector of low-wage or unemployed misery – is the medium term goal of the New Right'. And the 'more a dualistic economy and society is created, the stronger will be the roll-back pressure on the welfare state'.[81] In other words, the welfare state *is* proving reversible. What is more, reversibility seems to be quite compatible with liberal democracy and, indeed, the continuing electoral popularity of the New Right! To recognize this is also to acknowledge the central weakness of the irreversibility thesis – its monolithic approach which defines the situation in terms of two opposing social forces in conflict, with the conclusion that the forces defending the welfare state will prevail. Both the welfare state and the forces defending it are seen in undifferentiated terms. Piven and Cloward's formulation of the situation as 'capitalism against democracy' and of the latter's counter-attack in defence of the welfare state sums up this approach neatly.[82] Piven and Cloward were not unaware that Reagan's economic and social policies would impact somewhat differently on different social strata. However, they believed that the administration had tried to reverse 'so wide a range of federal policies' that 'opposition by an equally wide range of groups is inevitable'.[83] Instead of a situation of 'divide and rule' this would create a united front of strong opposition by groups adversely affected by Reagan policies. Interestingly, Piven and Cloward later took full account of the fact that, with the exception of unemployment insurance, universal programmes escaped largely unscathed while means-tested and other low-income programmes suffered substantial cuts. Overall, however – and, one might add, in keeping with their optimistic and activist persuasion – they have chosen to emphasize the failure of Reagan's attack on the welfare state rather than his success in scaling it down in part and in facilitating the development of a dual economy and society, a development which seems to have proceeded quite far in the United States. Similarly, Piven and Cloward fail to notice that it was not democracy as a whole that was pitted against capitalism but only parts of it; other parts were *with* capitalism. In sum, the major weakness of the irreversibility thesis lies in its failure to deal adequately with the implications for welfare state policy of the social stratification of capitalist society and the resulting fragmentation of group interests.

By the same token, the crucial divide between universal and selective services and its significance for the retrenchment of the welfare state have not been appreciated by many analysts. Thus Gilbert believes that it was the unprincipled 'drift' towards universality of the American welfare state during the 1960s and the early 1970s that led to the backlash of the 1980s.[84] Yet the strong support for universal entitlement programmes such as social security, the government's inability to retrench such programmes and, conversely, its far greater success in cutting back programmes for low-income groups suggest a very different conclusion. True, there was a rapid growth of social welfare expenditures and programmes in the United States which lacked a coherent rationale, for example of the 'welfare state'. There is also no doubt that it was largely a response to interest-group pressure. But, as the strong constituency for universal services in Britain and in many other countries shows, a clear philosophy of social expenditure does not seem to be a necessary condition for the defence of social programmes as long as they benefit the large majority of the population. It is in this context that the difference in the United States between the New Deal programmes (universal entitlement), on the one hand, and the Great Society programmes (selective 'welfare' assistance), on the other, seems crucial. Social scientists of varying persuasion, such as Brown, Navarro, Schorr and Weir, and Skocpol and Orloff, recognize this distinction very clearly, as they do the significance of universal programmes for sustaining support for social welfare.[85] Miller and Jenkins, too, while appealing to American 'social conscience' to alleviate poverty, recognize the need to broaden the base of social programmes.[86]

It is precisely in this context that the theses of Korpi and, in a different sense, LeGrand become relevant for understanding the impact of neo-conservative policies on the welfare state. Korpi has pointed out that universal social programmes benefit both the middle and working class and therefore have a strong constituency in their favour. As a result they are less vulnerable to retrenchment policies. On the other hand, residual programmes, which are means-tested and serve only a part of the working class, tend to divide the working class so that one sector sees itself as paying for another sector without enjoying any of the benefits. In this situation the middle class and large sections of the working class find themselves in a coalition against the 'poor'. Selective programmes therefore tend to be far more vulnerable to retrenchment.[87] Korpi's thesis has the merit of drawing attention to the differences between

social programmes and their relationship to stratification and the
politics of retrenchment. In a similar vein, albeit from a very
different theoretical perspective, LeGrand and Winter have also
argued that programmes which benefit the middle classes have a
much better chance of survival than those which do not. They have
found some support for this thesis in Britain for the period of 1978–9
to 1983–4.[88] LeGrand and Winter do not separate the programmes
which serve the *middle class only* from those that may be considered
'classless' or universal (such as health care and education). However, following Korpi, it is reasonable to suggest that programmes
which have a cross-class constituency would have even stronger
durability, given electoral considerations, than programmes which
serve only the middle class. Although LeGrand and Winter are
impressed by the durability of the British welfare state, which they
see almost entirely in terms of the size of public expenditure, their
analysis at least recognizes that parts of the welfare state, especially
those that serve the poor and powerless minorities such as the
unemployed and the lower working class (for example, public
housing) have been cut and are vulnerable to further cuts.[89] Had
LeGrand and Winter included unemployment and the changes in
taxation brought about by the Thatcher government in their
analysis, the class character of the New Right's public policies
would have become all the more evident. Finally, LeGrand and
Winter do not explore the prospect of a trade-off between tax
reduction and the retrenchment of public services for the middle
class (an eminently rational choice proposition) which seems to
underlie the Thatcherite project of moving social policy in a residual
direction. At any rate, in different ways both Korpi and LeGrand
and Winter draw attention to the differential retrenchment of the
welfare state, including the potential for it, and thus by implication
to the trend towards the dualization of society in countries such as
the United Kingdom and the United States.

## Conclusion

Neo-conservative governments in the United Kingdom and the
United States have followed economic, social, fiscal and labour-
relations policies that depart in significant ways from those followed
or entailed by the Keynesian welfare state. An exclusive focus on

universal programmes or on aggregate social expenditure conceals from view a whole host of changes that have significance from the standpoint of social inequality and the social well-being of individuals. Monetarism and unemployment, the retrenchment of programmes serving the lower working class and the poor, deregulation of conditions which protect the working poor (such as wages councils in Britain), the emasculation of trades unions, as well as massive tax reductions for the wealthy and for businesses with an increase in the tax burden of the poor, are some of these. Only by defining the parameters of the welfare state very narrowly and by taking a static view of the situation can one deny the significance of these changes for the welfare state and for the nature of societies being created by the New Right. Much of the change brought about by Reagan and Thatcher governments has been congruent with the ideology of the New Right – the *direction* of change has been quite unmistakable although the *magnitude* of change has in some respects been small. Social scientists, particularly in Britain, have often enough pointed out the vast gulf between the rhetoric of welfare state retrenchment and the reality of its persistence and even growth. In doing so they have left out the crucial intervening variable – the actual electoral platform and policy statements of neo-conservative parties (see pages 36–7 above). These have rarely proposed the retrenchment of universal social services, thanks largely to the continuing popularity of state welfare services in the face of the ideological onslaught mounted by the New Right. But an overemphasis on the ineffectiveness of the New Right in this respect has served to obscure the long-term strategy of retrenchment being followed by neo-conservative regimes as well as a range of developments directly or indirectly relevant to a reduction in social welfare.

## Notes and references

1. See, for example, Steinfels (1979); Bosanquet (1983); Levitas (1985); Barry (1987); and King (1987). In this book we use the term 'New Right' interchangeably with 'neo-conservative', no distinction being drawn between economic and social policies as such.
2. This view of the welfare state is an abstraction of the principles and institutions underlying the post-war British welfare state influenced by the ideas of J. M. Keynes and W. Beveridge. Briefly, it may be

described as the Keynesian welfare state, the target of neo-conservative ideological attack of the seventies especially in the United States and Britain. See Mishra (1984: chs 1 and 2).

3. It is virtually impossible to examine changes in the welfare state without some reference to inequality. However, income distribution and inequality *per se* will not be a focus of our interest. Regulatory measures, for example those concerned with occupational health and safety, environmental protection and human rights, though important for maintaining minimum standards of well-being, must also be left out of account. On the other hand, changes in taxation will be examined in some detail because tax policies have implications for the maintenance of social programmes as well as for equity and distributive justice more generally.

4. See Appendix 1, for a discussion of our definition of the 'welfare state'.

5. On unemployment, see OECD (1984a: 39). On trends in expenditure, see OECD (1985b: 18–23).

6. On Britain, see Gough (1979: 129–34). On the United States, see Ferguson and Rogers (1986: 80, 105–11). See also Ruggles and O'Higgins (1987: 160–1) and Krieger (1986: 92–3, 126–9).

7. OECD (1964: 110); OECD (1984a: 39).

8. OECD (1984a: 39); 'Jobless figure a record once again', *Manchester Guardian Weekly* (17 March 1985: 3).

9. Riddell (1985: 60, 248).

10. Apple (1980: 13–15, 29); Therborn (1986: 112–13).

11. OECD (1964: 82) and OECD (1984a: 39).

12. The average for 1974–9 was 6.7%, compared with 7% for 1986. See Tables 1 and 6, Appendix 2.

13. Thurow (1985: 12, 30); Mills (1984: 10–13); Navarro (1985: 44, 47).

14. OECD (1987a: 18).

15. On the United Kingdom, see Table 5, Appendix 2. See also J. Tobin, 'Monetarism: An ebbing tide?', *The Economist* (27 April 1985).

16. Loney (1986: 67–8).

17. Loney (1986: 69); Riddell (1985: 78–9); Labour Party Research Department (1985: 149).

18. Palmer and Sawhill (1984b: 378–9).

19. Ferguson and Rogers (1986: 137).

20. Ruggles and O'Higgins (1987: 165).

21. See, for example, Harrington (1984: 49–51).

22. Riddell (1985: 162–3, 239); Taylor-Gooby (1985: 29–32, 36–7); Lipset (1985); 'Attitudes of the American public towards social security', *International Social Security Review* (1986: 1, 72–3).

23. Riddell (1985: 131–5, 137).

24. Riddell (1985: 154–5); Taylor-Gooby (1987: 8)

25. Taylor-Gooby (1987: 4–5).

26. Loney (1986: 95, 104–10, 123–5); Riddell (1985: 149, 254–5); 'The starving of the NHS', *Manchester Guardian Weekly* (13 March 1988:

12); 'The NHS: A suitable case for much better treatment', *Manchester Guardian Weekly* (31 Januaary 1988: 6).
27. Taylor-Gooby (1987: 7, Table 2); 'The NHS: A suitable case for much better treatment', *Manchester Guardian Weekly* (31 January 1988: 6).
28. Zimbalist (1987: 19).
29. Zimbalist (1987: 19).
30. King (1987: 148–9); Loney (1986: 53–5); Palmer and Sawhill (1984a: 12–16); Salamon and Abramson (1984: 37–40); Lee Bawden and Palmer (1984: 177–9).
31. Mills (1984: 113); Lee Bawden and Palmer (1984: 184–7, 189–94).
32. Palmer and Sawhill (1984b: 376–7).
33. Abramovitz (1986: 259–60).
34. Loney (1986: 145).
35. Loney (1986: 147); Taylor-Gooby (1987: 8); 'Filed away in a cardboard box city', *Manchester Guardian Weekly* (29 May 1988: 22).
36. Labour Party Research Department (1985: 116–17); Brosnan and Wilkinson (1987: 14).
37. Those earning less than two-thirds of the average hourly earnings of male full-time workers are defined as low-paid. See Campling (1986: 374); Brosnan and Wilkinson (1987: 7).
38. Loney (1986: 104–5; 129); Labour Party Research Department (1985: 37).
39. Campling (1988: 525–6); 'More losers than gainers in social credit changes', *Manchester Guardian Weekly* (17 April 1988: 3); Campling (1989b: 419).
40. O'Higgins (1985: 301).
41. 'Growth of poverty', *Manchester Guardian Weekly* (29 May 1988: 3); Campling (1989a: 119). The poverty line in Britain refers to the level of social assistance benefits ('supplementary benefits') standardized nationally.
42. Bosanquet (1983: 113).
43. As Prime Minister Thatcher declared recently '[We] simply cannot delegate the exercise of mercy and generosity to others.' See 'Creation of wealth seen as a Christian duty', *Manchester Guardian Weekly* (29 May 1988: 12).
44. Palmer and Sawhill (1984a: 13).
45. Lee Bawden and Palmer (1984: 192).
46. Lee Bawden and Palmer (1984: 192).
47. Lee Bawden and Palmer (1984: 192).
48. Ferguson and Rogers (1986: 129).
49. Piven and Cloward (1987: 82).
50. Piven and Cloward (1987: 82).
51. 'Starvation stalks the US', *Manchester Guardian Weekly* (13 December 1987: 10).
52. Piven and Cloward (1987: 82).
53. US Bureau of the Census (1986: 442).

54. 'Starvation stalks the US', *Manchester Guardian Weekly* (13 December 1987: 10).
55. Riddell (1985: 62, 258); 'Budget for the rich', *Manchester Guardian Weekly* (27 March 1988: 4); 'Tory peers back poll tax', *Manchester Guardian Weekly* (29 May 1988: 3).
56. Riddell (1985: 71–2); Loney (1986: 64–5, 87).
57. Loney (1986: 104–5).
58. Loney (1986: 87).
59. 'Budget for the rich', *Manchester Guardian Weekly* (27 March 1988: 4).
60. 'Budget for the rich', *Manchester Guardian Weekly* (27 March 1988: 4).
61. Moon and Sawhill (1984: 325–6); Ferguson and Rogers (1986: 123).
62. Moon and Sawhill (1984: 324).
63. Moon and Sawhill (1984: 327). Taking social security and income taxes together and adjusting for inflation, it is estimated that taxes actually increased for those making less than $30,000 a year (with a 22% increase for those below $10,000 a year). On the other hand, for those making over $200,000 there was a reduction of 15% over the 1982–4 period. Effective tax rates for businesses were halved as a result of the 1981 tax changes. See Ferguson and Rogers (1986: 122–3).
64. Ferguson and Rogers (1986: 130).
65. Ruggles and O'Higgins (1987: 176).
66. Ruggles and O'Higgins (1987: 176).
67. Krieger (1987: 195). In case the President and the Congress disagree, an automatic process of budget cuts will go into effect. However, the main social programmes are exempt from this automatic process of cuts. For details, see Bell (1987: 251).
68. Offe (1984); Therborn (1984); Piven and Cloward (1985); LeGrand and Winter (1987); Ruggles and O'Higgins (1987).
69. LeGrand and Winter (1987: 148).
70. Piven and Cloward (1985: 157).
71. Piven and Cloward (1985: 158).
72. Ruggles and O'Higgins (1987: 187).
73. Therborn (1984: 28). See also Therborn and Roebroek (1986: 320–2).
74. Robinson (1986: 4).
75. Taylor-Gooby (1987: 21–7).
76. Taylor-Gooby (1987: 27).
77. Taylor-Gooby (1987: 27).
78. Ruggles and O'Higgins (1987: 187).
79. Palmer and Sawhill (1984a: 28–9).
80. See, for example, Harrison (1987: 6–10); Harrington and Levinson (1985: 417–26).
81. Therborn and Roebroek (1986: 335).
82. Piven and Cloward (1985: chs 1 and 5).
83. Piven and Cloward (1985: 139).

84. Gilbert (1983: 72–3, chs 3 and 4, *passim*).
85. Brown (1988); Navarro (1985); Schorr (1986); Weir *et al.* (1988).
86. Miller and Jenkins (1987: 57–8).
87. Korpi (1980: 305).
88. LeGrand and Winter (1987: 165–6).
89. LeGrand and Winter (1987: 148, 154).

# 3

# Social corporatism: defending the welfare state in Sweden and Austria

Sweden and Austria provide, perhaps, the two best-known and most successful examples of the approach we have called social corporatism. What kinds of policies have these regimes followed? To what extent have they been successful in defending and even consolidating the post-war welfare state? Has the defence of social welfare been at the cost of the economic well-being of the country? These questions form the nucleus of our investigation in this chapter. As in the previous chapter, here also we review policies under three headings: full employment; universal social services; and the maintenance of basic minimum standards. This review is followed by an examination of two basic arguments: first, that social-corporatist arrangements benefit well-organized economic groups represented within decision-making structures to the detriment of others; and second, that the system is disintegrating as the 'social partnership' and consensus underlying it begin to crumble.

## Maintaining full employment

A recent study of unemployment in Western industrial countries concludes that countries with an 'institutionalized commitment' to the goal of full employment have successfully attained this goal in the face of severe economic problems since the early 1970s. That these countries include Sweden and Austria is not surprising. Indeed, of the four European countries singled out in that study, three are corporatist social democracies in our sense of the term.[1]

## Sweden

Down to the early 1970s Sweden's strategy of full employment was based chiefly on a combination of an anti-cyclical investment policy and an active labour-market policy under the direction of the Labour Market Board. The Swedish Labour Market Board is formally a tripartite body which consists of representatives of the government, the employers' and workers' organizations. In effect, the major partners are workers' and employers' organizations. Counter-cyclical investment planning has basically meant a series of incentives and controls which encourage firms to set aside profits as reserve funds to be invested in times of recession. The labour market policy involves extensive training and relocation programmes for workers as well as public works schemes. Indeed, labour redundancy from marginal and declining industries has been actively encouraged – a distinctive feature of Swedish policy. Through its well-developed and generous programme of retraining and, if necessary, relocation, it has been possible to move workers out of low-paid and declining industries into better-paid, modern sectors of the economy. Sweden has tried to combine the objective of higher productivity and full employment with that of 'wage solidarity' or the reduction of wage differentials within the labour force. In this way Sweden has managed successfully to address certain dysfunctional tendencies of full-employment capitalism, for example overmanning, labour rigidity and low productivity. The inability of the British welfare state to address these weaknesses of welfare capitalism effectively was one of its main failures.

Apart from its labour market policy, a second major feature of the Swedish approach towards harmonizing the economic and social goals of the welfare state has been a centralized system of wage bargaining at the national level between the employers' organization (Svenska Arbetsgivareföreningen) and the main workers' organisation (Landsorganisationen).[2] The annual wage bargain is generally based on a carefully calculated estimate of the increase in the national income. A broad framework of agreement outlining the principle of wage settlement is arrived at and individual industry agreements are then negotiated by the two sides within the framework laid down at the national level. We may describe it as both a voluntary and a national wages or incomes policy. On the one hand, this approach helps contain inflation – a major post-war problem of full-employment capitalism – and, on the other hand, it also helps maintain the goal of 'wage solidarity' since free-for-all collective bargaining inevitably leads to greater wage disparity. Overall, the Swedish approach to wage negotiations has been based on the appreciation of two things: the importance of wage moderation in conditions of full employment and close interdependence and, therefore, the possibility of trade-offs between social and economic policies which involve full employment, inflation, economic growth, social welfare and economic wages. Indeed, this type of 'societal bargaining' (in Walter Korpi's phrase) between capital and labour also introduces an element of 'planning' into the economy which allows for a measure of stability and control.[3] A comparison of inflation rates between Sweden and Britain underscores the point. During the difficult years of 1975–9 inflation in Sweden averaged 9.7%, compared with 15.6% in Britain and 11% in OECD Europe. The significance of these figures becomes clearer when we note that during these years unemployment in Sweden was a mere 1.9%, compared with 5.4% in the UK and 5.4% in OECD Europe (see Table 5, Appendix 2).

In short, a 'socially responsible' approach to the management of welfare capitalism has been the main feature of the Swedish model. Through an institutionalized process of national collective bargaining and cooperation through the Labour Market Board, the major economic groups in industrial capitalism (workers and employers) have been made to assume responsibility for broader national objectives. In this way social corporatism has sought to harmonize production with distribution and economic with social welfare in order to maintain the basic preconditions and institutions of the welfare state.

Down to the early 1970s the Swedish system worked very well in combining full employment and economic growth with a generous and expanding system of social welfare. The oil-price shock of 1973, however, brought in its train the problem of stagflation. In the mid-1970s Swedish industries such as iron-mining, steel, shipbuilding and forestry were hit hard by the international recession. Because of the deep and prolonged nature of the recession and the collapse of demand, normal anti-cyclical measures and labour-market policies could not stem the tide of potential redundancies and unemployment. Sweden therefore supplemented its traditional employment policies with several other measures.[4] Prominent among these were the following.

First, labour-market policy was expanded from being largely a means of facilitating labour mobility to a means of providing substitute employment in regions with surplus labour. Second, the government provided very substantial grants (subsidies and loans) to industry. The objectives were twofold: first, to help industries hit by the recession to restructure and adapt; and second, to encourage firms to maintain production and avoid large-scale redundancies. Compared with the first half of the 1970s, expenditure on these grants during the second half rose fivefold.[5] Meanwhile public sector employment was also expanded. In addition, certain other measures such as early retirement were put into effect. As a result, public expenditure as a percentage of GDP rose from 48% in 1974 to 58% in 1977 and to 67% in 1982 (cf. the United Kingdom's expenditure of 45% in 1974, 44% in 1977 and 47% in 1982).[6] The budget balance, which was in surplus for the best part of the 1970s, went into deficit in 1978 and by 1982 the general government deficit rose to 6.3% of GDP.[7] In other words, the severity and duration of the economic dislocation of the 1970s took a heavy toll. By the mid-1980s, however, Sweden had bounced back economically and, overall, Swedish industry adapted successfully to new conditions. Most of the government subsidies to industry have since been phased out. Traditional labour-market measures remain in place, albeit now with a larger job-creation component. In 1987 labour-market policies accounted for about 4% of the labour force while unemployment stood at 1.9%. Inflation was down to 4.2% and the 1986 deficit was a mere 0.7% of GDP.[8] As Table 5 in Appendix 2 shows, in 1975–9 Sweden's economic growth fell below that of OECD Europe but by 1980–4 it averaged 1.6% against Europe's 1.1%. For 1980–8 Sweden's growth rate of 1.8% was virtually identical with that of OECD Europe (calculated from OECD, 1988b: 170).[9] Clearly, Sweden seems to have come through the acute crisis induced by the OPEC price rises of 1973 and 1979 and the depressions of 1975 and 1982 without sacrificing a basic ingredient of the post-war welfare state – full employment.

### Austria

Austria shares with Sweden a strong national commitment to full employment dating back to the early 1960s. Admittedly, the institutions of 'social partnership' are very different from Sweden's system of national bargaining. Nevertheless, they embody the same basic principle of harmonizing economic and social policies through voluntary agreement among major producer interests, i.e. capital and labour. Austrian 'social partnership', however, represents a far more strongly institutionalized form of social consensus.[10] The Joint Commission on Wages and Prices, one of the most important institutions of social partnership, was set up in 1957. The impetus behind this move was the post-war objective of achieving economic and political stability. Four economic partner organizations, covering agriculture, industry and labour, are responsible for running the Joint Commission. It works through committees responsible for wages, prices and economic and social questions, respectively. Government representatives attend the Commission's meetings but have no voting rights. In any case the Commission is not so much a forum for the representation of interests as a corporate body which seeks to arrive at a consensus and make unanimous decisions. Wage policies and recommendations of the Commission have no legal standing and wage moderation is less a function of centrally established guidelines than of a climate of opinion created by the social partnership and other consensus-making bodies.

Social partnership is based on the recognition that consensus among major economic groupings – chiefly employers and workers – is a prerequisite for the smooth functioning of a modern industrial market economy. In particular, it is recognized that if social policy objectives such as full employment and social welfare are to be achieved, economic policy issues must be addressed. More generally, the interdependence of economic and social objectives is acknowledged and the relationship, including the trade-off between economic wages and social welfare, wages and inflation, and inflation and unemployment, forms the basis of the general policy approach. In effect Austria has a form of permanent incomes and prices policy voluntarily arrived at by major economic interests and closely related to a set of agreed national objectives of which full employment and economic growth are the most important.

In the 1960s unemployment in Austria was less than 2%, as indeed it was in most industrial countries of Western Europe. Austria's full-employment policies were not really put to the test until after the OPEC price shock and the ensuing stagflation. How did Austria cope with inflation and the economic recession of the 1970s? Put simply, the social consensus approach made it possible to contain inflation through wage moderation which, in turn, allowed a Keynesian-style reflationary policy to be adopted without the fear of inflationary consequences. That, in essence, was the Austrian approach to maintaining full employment.[11] This, however, meant deficit financing. Austria's budget balance, which until 1974 was in surplus, went into a sizeable deficit in 1975 (see Table 4, Appendix 2). Swedish-style labour-market policy has not been a feature of the Austrian approach and so such measures have played only a minor part in helping sustain employment. On the other hand, nationalized industries and enterprises form a significant part of Austria's economy. The government encouraged the public sector to retain labour in order to prevent unemployment from rising. Further, as in Sweden, albeit on a more modest scale, substantial assistance in the form of grants and loans was provided to both private and public sectors in order to help industry maintain investment and employment.[12] From about 1974 the number of foreign workers was also reduced. Although this helped cut unemployment by about half, it must be remembered that the outflow of 'guestworkers' was to some extent counter-balanced by the return of Austrian workers from West Germany.[13] A variety of other measures, such as a shorter working week and early retirement, were also put in place to ease unemployment. During 1975–9 unemployment averaged 1.9%, inflation 5.7%, economic growth 2.7% and the budget deficit 2.7% of GDP. Corresponding figures for OECD Europe were 5.4%, 11%, 2.7% and 3.3% (see Table 5, Appendix 2). Clearly, the 1970s proved a very successful period for the Austrian welfare state, with unemployment remaining below 2%.

The 1980s, however, saw an increase in the rate of unemployment. Although a good deal lower than the OECD Europe average, it is high by Austrian standards. After the world recession of 1982, Austria's budget deficit rose sharply – from 1.7% of GDP in 1981 to 4.0% in 1983 (see Table 4, Appendix 2). This marked the beginning of a shift in priority to reducing the deficit; it was felt that the Keynesian-style reflationary measures and other employment-support measures used in the 1970s could not be repeated. Yet keeping unemployment low remains a high priority for Austrian social policy and it is likely that, in future, labour-market measures such as job retraining, relocation and public works will play a bigger part. In any case, an average unemployment rate of 3.2% for 1980–4 and

3.5% for 1985–7 is a considerable achievement, compared with the OECD European average of 9.8% for 1980–4 and 10.9% for 1985–7.[14]

In sum, like Sweden, Austria also succeeded in maintaining full employment through the 1970s and near-full employment in the 1980s, thanks largely to institutionalized cooperation among major interests. This enabled various trade-offs between employment and wage moderation to be worked out and major economic and social goals to be achieved within the framework of a broad consensus. Moreover, Table 5, Appendix 2, tells its own story in terms of other economic indices. Full employment does not seem to have been achieved at the price of economic growth or inflation.

## Universal social services

Compared with full employment, the task of maintaining the framework and level of universal social services has been easier in both Sweden and Austria. This is not surprising when we consider that even neo-conservative regimes in the United States and the United Kingdom have been unwilling or unable thus far to make substantial changes in universal entitlement programmes. During 1975–81 Sweden's real social expenditure grew annually by 4.0% and Austria's by 4.4%. The corresponding growth rates in the United States and Britain were 2.8% and 2.5%, respectively, while the average for OECD countries was 4.3%.[15] Indeed, as we have seen, public expenditure, including social expenditure, increased in these countries through the 1970s. This is particularly true of Sweden, whose social expenditure as a proportion of GDP rose from 26.9% in 1975 to 33.4% in 1981. In the United States, by contrast, social expenditure as a percentage of GDP remained constant at 20.8% over the same period.[16] Under the Reagan administration social expenditure was held down, although *public* expenditure as a proportion of GDP actually rose largely due to the vast growth in military spending.[17]

In Sweden proposals for moving away from universal services and relying more on the private sector came from the non-socialist parties which held office during 1976–81. Social Democrats were opposed to this policy and in 1982 campaigned for the maintenance and consolidation of universal social programmes. With the exception of child-care services, however, no further expansion of social welfare was envisaged. Social Democrats won, as indeed they did in the two successive elections in 1985 and 1988 on broadly the same platform as far as social policy was concerned.[18] Currently they are in office with Communist Party support.

In the 1970s social programmes and expenditures grew a good deal in Sweden. Many of the relevant initiatives had been planned earlier in less troubled times with the expectation that the recession would be short-lived.[19] In the 1980s the economic climate was very different. Social Democrats now aimed at consolidation and improvement rather than expansion of the welfare state. For the best part of the 1980s the government followed a tight budgetary policy and tried to ease the tax burden of the most highly taxed people in the world. The 1980s also saw some cutbacks in expenditures, especially in housing.[20]

Austrian developments largely parallel those of Sweden. The 1970s were a period of growth in social services based in part on the expectation that the recession, and therefore the need to resort to a budget deficit, would not be prolonged. These expectations proved unrealistic and the 1980s brought a period of relative austerity.[21] Reducing the budget deficit and maintaining high levels of employment are major goals, although, unlike Sweden, the goal of full employment has been increasingly compromised. This change in policy has been described as one from 'full employment at all costs' to 'high employment at affordable costs'.[22] Austria has tried to maintain the level of services by raising contributions, for example in the case of pensions. Since 1983, partly due to political changes, budgetary policy has involved cutbacks in social spending, reductions in some benefits (such as pensions) and improvements in others.[23] Overall, however, the basic approach to social benefits has been that existing entitlements should not be reduced. In other words, the policy objective has been to maintain the network of universal services and not to resort to selectivity and privatization. On the other hand, further real growth in social programmes and expenditures is considered unlikely.[24]

## Poverty and basic minimum standards

The recent increase in poverty in the United States and in the United Kingdom, resulting largely from unemployment and the retrenchment of social benefits, shows clearly the role of full employment and social services in preventing poverty and maintaining minimum standards. Given the creditable record of Sweden and Austria in respect of these, basic minimum standards are likely to be maintained. Furthermore, it appears that, in so far as cutbacks have been made, the social-consensus approach has allowed a more equitable across-the-board reduction.[25] This is in clear contrast to the politically expedient reductions in the United Kingdom and especially in the United States which have mainly hit the poor. For all these reasons, then, the third characteristic of the welfare state – commitment to a national minimum standard of living – also remains largely intact in Sweden and Austria.

It should be noted, however, that poverty statistics along the lines of those provided by the United States and the United Kingdom are not available for Sweden and Austria, which makes comparison somewhat difficult. Both countries rely mainly on universal entitlement programmes for the prevention of poverty; means-tested assistance has played only a marginal role. However, Swedish data show that the proportion of the population dependent on social assistance increased from around 4.5% in the late 1970s to over 6% in the mid-1980s, suggesting a rise in the low-income population despite the preventive efforts noted above. It appears that an increase in the number of long-term unemployed and also of single-parent families are important reasons for this.[26] In Austria social assistance, which is provided by the provinces and municipalities, has not formed a major part of the social welfare system. In 1983 only 0.4% of the population was receiving cash assistance.[27] To what extent the number of Austrians on social assistance has increased is not known. But long-term unemployment is sure to increase the number of poor. Finally, we should point out that, unlike neo-conservative regimes, neither Sweden nor Austria has made any significant change in the tax system which would result in an upward redistribution of income and income inequality.[28]

## Social corporatism: a critical assessment

We have argued so far that social corporatism has successfully maintained the post-war welfare state and pro-labour social policies in the face of serious difficulties stemming from the dislocations of the international economy. However, nagging questions still re-

main. These concern the equity as well as the stability of the system.
Let us consider these in turn.

## Bias towards organized interests

It has been suggested by sceptics that tripartism is a form of
power-sharing among large-scale organized producer interests
engaged in peak-level bargaining. The interests of these powerful
organized groups are well taken care of but at the expense of those
unrepresented at the bargaining table – non-producer groups and
other less well-organized sectors of society. The implication is that,
while maintaining the broad framework of the welfare state,
corporatist arrangements are likely to promote inequality and to
curtail rather than enhance democracy. They are also likely to
create a form of consensus society managed by a small elite and
unresponsive to the wishes and interests of the masses. According
to one critic: 'Corporatist arrangements are inherently inequitable.
Moreover by definition they exclude representation of many
interests. *Their most common outcome is to shift the costs of
decisions onto those who do not have a place at the table*' (italics
mine).[29]

Others have expressed the fear that corporatist strategies may
'facilitate low-visibility control of resources on behalf of the
privileged'.[30] Ethnic minorities, unskilled workers, the elderly,
youth, and the disabled could, for example, be marginalized or
excluded from the incorporation process and their needs ignored.
Echoing these misgivings, a left-wing critic writes that the social
contract underlying corporatism is likely to be 'between capital and
an *unreconstructed* working class. The interests and politics of
women, Blacks, youths, the elderly and the disabled, who have no
corporate base from which to strike a deal with capital are likely to
be marginalised'.[31]

These misgivings about corporatism have to be taken seriously. A
part of the problem here is with the different ways in which the term
'corporatism' is understood and used in analysis. There are similar if
less serious problems with the meaning ascribed to the 'welfare
state'.

In this book corporatism is understood essentially as tripartism at
the *societal* level which seeks to achieve trade-offs between various

economic and social objectives in light of the overall national situation.[32] The concept of the welfare state as understood here includes the maintenance of full employment. This is a point of some importance. Most writers on social welfare equate the welfare state with state programmes and activities which provide a range of basic social services and transfer payments. State policies for maintaining full employment are not normally seen as a part of the welfare state. Yet maintaining full employment has been a major objective of social corporatism for which the principal trade-off has been voluntary wage restraint. Critics of corporatism fail to take into account this major objective and achievement of welfare corporatism. Moreover, the view of corporatism as simply a form of representation of producer interests fails to appreciate its class character (see Chapter 1). This is a point which will be taken up in a subsequent chapter. For the moment, I would like to examine the concern voiced by critics about the interests of non-producers and other social groups unrepresented at the bargaining table. Let us leave aside general arguments for and against this view, and consider the implications of some of the major policies pursued by social-corporatist regimes.

The hallmark of social corporatism such as practised by Sweden and Austria has been a determined effort to maintain full employment, an effort that has met with considerable success. Assuming that the social-contract approach helps to keep unemployment down, what are the implications for groups singled out by critics as excluded from the bargaining table and therefore likely to be marginalized? Such groups include ethnic minorities, unskilled workers, youths, the elderly, the disabled, female-headed families – and one might add, women in general. It seems that, with respect to jobs at least, far from being detrimental to the interests of these groups, social corporatism is in fact the very opposite. Evidence shows quite clearly that unemployment affects these groups disproportionately. It follows that a policy of maintaining full employment is particularly beneficial to these groups who, in an open-market situation, are much more likely to be unemployed. It is important to remember, however, that 'full employment' should not be at the cost of excluding ethnic minorities, youths and others from the labour market in a way that is detrimental to their interest. There is no evidence to suggest that either in Sweden or Austria full employment has been achieved at the cost of the job prospects of any of the above groups. (The question of 'guestworkers' in Austria is discussed below.)

However, it is also the case that regimes which may be social-democratic and corporatist nevertheless differ in the extent to which they pursue equitable social policies. Thus Sweden has pursued the policy of 'wage solidarity', i.e. the attempt to narrow the gap between the highest- and lowest-paid blue-collar workers, whereas Austria has not. This is in part due to the fact that social democracy has been a stronger force in Sweden than in Austria.[33] The wage differential between youth and adult workers shows a similar picture. In Sweden the ratio of the average youth wage to the adult wage for blue-collar jobs rose from 56% in 1960 to almost 75% in the 1980s.[34] Nothing of the kind seems to have happened in Austria, where young workers (for example, apprentices) are paid a good deal less than adult workers.[35]

True, since about the mid-1970s Austria has reduced the number of foreign workers admitted to the country. But neither the scale nor the speed of the restriction suggests a xenophobic move.[36] In somewhat differing ways, both Austria and Sweden, the latter following more equitable policies overall, have waged a sustained battle against unemployment since about the mid-1970s. The 'Social Contract' of the 1970s in Britain, also meant to fight unemployment, provides a glaring contrast. Indeed the plight of non-whites, youths and unskilled workers generally in neo-conservative regimes such as the United Kingdom and the United States underlines the importance of full employment for the life chances of such minority groups. When we add to this regional and geographical disparity in the distribution of unemployment, the implications of a full-employment policy for preventing the decline and decimation of local communities become obvious.[37]

The same basic error – a priori reasoning which fails to examine the consequences of corporatism empirically – is made by critics of corporatism who see it simply or even primarily as a form of privileged representation of the interests of the well organized and the powerful. In fact the entire rationale of corporatism, at least in its voluntary, social-democratic version, is to move away from the pursuit of sectional interests, whether in respect of wages or the protection of employment, towards consideration of broad societal aggregates such as employment levels, inflation, economic growth, investment and social wage levels which concern the general population rather than specific groups. At any rate, it is reasonable to conclude that in promoting full employment, corporatism serves the interests of those who are marginal to the labour market or have weaker bargaining power far more than any conceivable alternative system of representation of interests is capable of doing in a capitalist society. (See, however, page 88 below on Australia.) A similar, though perhaps somewhat weaker, case could be made with respect to an incomes policy and centralized wage negotiations, key features of social corporatism.

It is generally recognized that incomes policies do not affect the share of wage-earners (that is, their wages as a whole) in the national income in the long run, although they may reduce it in the short run. On the other hand, incomes policies are known to reduce wage differentials, usually by raising the wages of the low-paid relative to others.[38] While empirical studies are not conclusive on causal relations, there is ample evidence to suggest that this is what happened, for example, in Britain during the 'Social Contract' of the late 1970s. In Sweden centralized wage negotiations, together with labour-market measures, have been crucial in reducing wage differentials among blue-collar workers as well as between blue-collar and white-collar workers. Indeed, one of the major problems of centralized wage bargaining and incomes policies is to persuade highly skilled and well-organized sections of the labour force to accept a narrower wage differential than they might otherwise obtain. Moreover, it is clear that such things as food subsidies, a higher 'social wage' and low inflation are to the advantage of all rather than the 'big battalions' of organized workers. In sum, two of the main policies associated with social-democratic corporatism – full employment and voluntary wage restraint – do not seem to harm the unorganized and the unrepresented and, indeed, work in their favour. Tables 8, 9 and 10, in Appendix 2, present data relevant to the position of those not 'represented' in corporate decision-making. Data on Austria are somewhat harder to come by. Where possible, therefore, data on Norway, which is generally acknowledged as a Scandinavian corporatist social democracy similar to Sweden, have been included. While pluralist liberal democracies may claim in principle that they provide more scope for interest representation to various marginalized groups, in reality such groups have fared much better under a system of 'societal bargaining'.

### The crumbling of the consensus?

The evidence adduced in the previous pages shows the success of social corporatism in Sweden and Austria in maintaining and defending the welfare state. Economic indicators also offer prima-facie evidence that the defence of national minimum standards has not been at the cost of economic efficiency. Clearly, maintaining full employment in particular has demanded the greatest determination and ingenuity on the part of these regimes. Yet over a period of time and given the support of the labour force and the cooperation of employers, commitment to both economic change and social protection has been honoured. The system has survived the consequences of two oil-price shocks (in 1973 and 1979) and the resulting recessions, and, at least in the case of Sweden, has also accommodated a sizeable restructuring of industry.[39] Does this, however, mean that the 'crisis' is over and that it is business as usual as far as social-democratic corporatism is concerned? Let us consider this question in some detail.

In a recent survey of tripartite experience, Leo Panitch writes of Austria and Sweden: 'It will be said, and rightly, that their performance is still better than the mass unemployment and assault on democratic rights (social rights and union rights) that is visible in other countries in the crisis.'[40] However, he adds: 'the point is that the instability and contradictions of the old social democratic tripartite option are accelerating; it is not a static and stable option'.[41] Panitch is right on both counts. He recognizes that, relatively speaking, these countries have done well in protecting employment (he is not concerned with the social expenditures and programmes of these and other countries); at the same time, he draws attention to the precarious nature of tripartite arrangements. Clearly tripartism is no panacea for the ills of capitalism. In no way can it transcend the inherent contradictions and conflicts of welfare capitalism.

Indeed, as Korpi, for example, insists, tripartism or corporatism is best understood as a part of, or rather a moment in, the ongoing class conflict between capital and labour.[42] It represents one form in which labour can exert political leverage in its endemic conflict with capital. This rules out stability or indeed any ultimate guarantees. Moreover, as many observers have pointed out, in liberal societies tipartism seems largely a function of large and centralized trade-union federations and a strong social-democratic party.[43] It is labour rather than capital that favours corporatism. This is especially the case in situations when there is a recession and when growth falters. As the period after the mid-1970s shows, capital has been able to use the market and free collective bargaining as a very effective weapon against labour. No wonder that in Sweden, for example, it is capital that has been far more interested in scuttling the centralized bargaining system, 'wage solidarity' and the consensus mode of operation, rather than labour.[44] In Austria, too, the pressure to move social policy in a more conservative direction (i.e. towards higher unemployment, privatization and social expenditure cuts) has increased as non-socialist parties have made electoral gains in recent years and as social democrats have lost their dominant position.[45] It could be that, given its strong institutionalization, Austria's 'social partnership' may endure for quite a while even as its policies turn increasingly away from the full-employment social welfare state of the past. But in the absence of a quid pro quo, the institutionalization of social partnership itself is unlikely to survive in the long run. Such a development is by no means unlikely. This is precisely where the role of democratic class struggle and social struggle more generally becomes clear. The very precariousness of tripartism and the systemic bias of capitalism towards free-market solutions underlines the importance of ideological and political struggle in the defence of the welfare state. In this context what is impressive is the fact that, since 1973, commitment to the welfare state has been maintained and the institutional integration of economic and social policy – the hallmark of both the Swedish and Austrian welfare state – has thus far remained largely intact. All the same, it cannot be denied that social-democratic tripartism, in its institutional aspect as well as in its capacity to integrate welfare capitalism, looks weaker today. Let us look at Sweden first.

### Sweden

The three main pillars of Swedish corporatism may be said to be: centralized wage bargaining and orderly labour relations (i.e. very few strikes); labour-market policies; and a general consensus over economic and social measures concerning the welfare state. How have these fared? Throughout the 1980s industrial relations in general and centralized bargaining in particular have had a difficult time. The fall of the Social Democratic government in 1976 strengthened the hands of employers and weakened the restraint usually exercised by unions when a socialist government is in office. In 1980 there was a major strike followed by a lock-out by employers. In 1983 the engineering workers (Swedish Metalworkers' Union) signed a separate agreement with their employers. The following year saw a further weakening of the centralized pattern of wage bargaining. With the growing numbers and importance of white-collar workers, especially public employees, inter-union rivalry has increased in recent years and coordination of collective bargaining has become more difficult.[46] As one trade unionist put it: 'Over the past few years bargaining has been in disarray and in the last analysis, unprofitable to all parties.'[47] He believes, however, that pressures for a 'return to co-ordinated central negotiations will prevail'.[48]

Sweden's labour-market policies not only remain in place but have expanded since the mid-1970s, and currently account for some 4% of the labour force. Naturally, expenditure on these policies has gone up.[49] However, in many ways labour-market policy may be the most enduring and 'exportable' part of Swedish welfare capitalism. Its important role in creating labour flexibility and in facilitating adaptation to technical change has been underlined by the recent shift in industrial economies from the production of goods to the provision of services and the growth of high-technology industries. Even *The Economist*, scarcely a pro-socialist journal, has had to admit that Swedish labour-market policy appears to be a good deal more effective than the alternative approach of relying on market forces and on unemployment to encourage the redeployment of labour.[50] It may well be that the Swedish model of industrial restructuring, which bypasses the classical market-oriented approach of the United States (relying on large numbers of small high-technology sweatshops and other low-paid service enterprises), could take on a new and strategic significance at this point in transition from manufacturing to service industries.[51]

What of the general consensus in favour of high social expenditure (and its corollary, high taxation) and the continuation of welfare state policies? The first thing to note here is that in Sweden, despite a very substantial rise in taxation, including personal taxation, there has been little overt tax–welfare backlash. While high taxation is resented, nearly two-thirds of the population in 1984 agreed that the public sector should be retained at its present level or even expanded. Three-quarters of those polled thought that state intervention was required to correct injustices which arise in market societies such as Sweden. [52] True, in the 1980s Social Democrats no less than conservatives favoured reducing marginal tax rates on incomes. Thus it was decided to lower the top rate from 87% to 77% and to reduce the rates so that for the vast majority of income earners the marginal rate would not exceed 50% (see also Table 7, Appendix 2).[53] On welfare state policies public opinion surveys in Sweden, in common with many other countries, show little change over the years. While there is evidence of greater polarization of opinion along party-political lines, there is little evidence of a drop in support for the welfare state.[54] Are the young less enamoured of social paternalism? In 1983 a survey of young people aged 18–24 in a number of Western countries found that no less than 62% of Swedes singled out the social welfare system as the feature of their country they were most proud of, compared with 42% in the United Kingdom and 31% in West Germany.[55] With more than half of Sweden's GDP taken away in taxes and with social expenditure in excess of 30% of GDP, support for the welfare state remains largely intact. Controversial features concern such new measures as wage-earners' funds. The non-socialist parties are pledged to their repeal, but that is unlikely to have a major impact on the practice of social welfare. Overall, however, we may accept the conclusion of a Swedish commentator that in the 1980s 'differences between parties and interest organizations have increased and what seemed to be a consensus on the Swedish model has partly withered away'.[56]

### Austria

We shall examine Austria along similar lines, that is, with respect to centralized wage bargaining and labour relations, tax–welfare backlash and the erosion of general economic and social consensus.

As we have noted already, 'social partnership' in Austria – the Chamber system of representation and the Wages Commission – is far more strongly institutionalized than it is in Sweden. Thus far there is little evidence to suggest that the system of centralized wage negotiations which includes the acceptance of general wage guide-lines has weakened in any way. Unlike in Sweden, there has not so far been any major disruption of industrial relations. As far as tax–welfare backlash is concerned, let us note first of all that the level of taxation in Austria is not particularly high.[57] None the less, conservatives have taken up the issue of taxation from the viewpoint of wasteful public expenditure. In 1984 73% of the population considered preventing wasteful spending of tax revenue as an urgent issue, compared with 56% in 1980. Concern with full employment and job security remains high, but in 1983 more than four-fifths of the population apparently believed that a reduction in public spending would help revitalize the private sector, which could create jobs.[58]

It has to be noted, however, that unlike their Swedish counterparts, social democrats in Austria have willingly or otherwise let unemployment rise to a level not experienced since the 1950s. As a result, social democracy is no longer perceived as a guarantor of employment as it used to be.[59] Meanwhile, the conservative insistence that the budget deficit must be reduced has become influential, with its inevitable implications for taxation and expenditure cuts. The current coalition government of conservative and social-democratic parties suggests stability and continuity with previous policies. But there is little doubt that priorities are shifting away from that of jobs and social welfare towards a pro-capitalist policy of higher unemployment, expenditure cuts, tax reduction and the reduction of budget deficits.[60] The influence of ideology and politics on social policy is quite evident within the framework of Austrian corporatism.

## Conclusion

A review of the nature and consequences of social corporatism in Sweden and Austria does not support the notion that it enhances the interests of the well-organized and producer groups at the cost of others. While it is clear that the welfare state is not necessarily an instrument of egalitarianism, for example in respect of patriarchy and gender relations, there are no good grounds to suggest that corporatist arrangements *per se* introduce an inegalitarian bias. Indeed, the experience of Sweden at least suggests the opposite. Overall, the evidence from Sweden and Austria shows that while corporatist institutions help sustain the welfare state, the nature of social and economic policies, for example with respect to redistribution and inequality of gender and race, followed by a corporatist welfare state depends on other factors.[61]

The experience of these two social-corporatist regimes since the oil-price shock of 1973 indicates that contradictions of welfare capitalism need not result in the breakdown of corporatist institutions. As a model of an advanced welfare state, social corporatism has weathered the storm in the 1970s and 1980s without sacrificing economic effectiveness and social justice. But it would be foolish to claim historical inevitability for either its continuation or its decline and fall. Factors favourable as well as unfavourable for the survival of social corporatism are at work. The situation must be seen in terms of an ongoing conflict and compromise in which, by and large, labour is likely to struggle for the retention of these arrangements while capital seeks to scuttle them in favour of a return to the market.

## Notes and references

1.   Therborn (1986: 16, 23).
2.   See Jones (1976: ch. 4); Albage (1986).
3.   Korpi (1983: 20).
4.   Henning (1984).
5.   Henning (1984: 200).
6.   OECD (1988a: 183).
7.   OECD (1988a: 182).
8.   OECD (1987c: 17); Tables 1, 3 and 4, pages 125–8.
9.   Calculated from OECD (1988a: 170).
10.   See OECD (1981: 29–40).
11.   See, for example, Martin (1986: 201–9); Seidel (1982); OECD (1982a: 22, 47).
12.   Martin (1986: 206–7); OECD (1983: 46–9).
13.   Martin (1986: 206); OECD (1983: 42–3).
14.   Calculated from OECD (1988a: 187).
15.   OECD (1985a: 28).
16.   OECD (1985a: 40, 72).
17.   Public expenditure rose from 34% of GDP in 1981 to 36.9% in 1986. OECD (1988a: 183).
18.   Olsson (1987: 86–9); 'Sweden: Still shining', *The Economist* (24 September 1988).
19.   Marklund (1988: 30, 41–3); Einhorn and Logue (1982: 15, 33).
20.   Marklund (1988: 30, 41–3); OECD (1982c: 35); Walters (1985: 359, 368–9).

21. Martin (1986: 208–9); Busch *et al.* (1986: 183, 189).
22. Münz and Wintersberger (1987: 239).
23. Busch *et al.* (1986: 189); Münz and Wintersberger (1987: 215, 228–9).
24. Busch *et. al.* (1986: 188–9).
25. See, for example, Walters (1985: 361, 368–9).
26. Marklund (1988: 52–5); Olsson (1987: 61–2).
27. Münz and Wintersberger (1987: 230).
28. Taxes and contributions taken together do show some decline in progressivity in both Austria and Sweden. For example, in Sweden the share of income taxes in the total tax revenue declined substantially in the 1970s while the share of employer's social security contribution (a less progressive tax) increased. It must be remembered, however, that in both countries (especially Sweden) total taxes as a percentage of GDP rose substantially. On Sweden see OECD (1985a: 58–9); on Sweden and Austria, see OECD (1987d: 83, 87, 91). Recent tax reforms in Sweden, unlike those in the United States and United Kingdom, aim at an equitable reduction in marginal tax rates. For example, in the United States the top marginal rate of income tax was reduced from 75% to 38%, in Britain from 83% to 60% (further reduced to 40% in 1988), whereas Austria's rate remained unchanged at 62% and Sweden's dropped from 88% to 77%. See Hagemann *et al.* (1988: 208).
29. Ferris (1985: 69).
30. Harrison (1984: 12).
31. Deacon (1985–6: 8).
32. This was also the sense in which the term was used in Mishra (1984: ch. 4). Some critics have equated corporatism with giving trade unions more say in the running of social services (a complete travesty of the idea of societal corporatism!) See Hyde and Deacon (1986–7: 19).
33. 'Sweden's economy', *The Economist* (7 March 1987).
34. 'Sweden's economy', *The Economist* (7 March 1987).
35. Butschek (1982: 110, 125).
36. From 112,000 in 1970 it rose to a peak of 227,000 in 1973 and then declined to 175,000 in 1980. See OECD (1983: 43). In 1970 foreign workers constituted 4.7% of the labour force, in 1973 8.7% and in 1980 6.3%. Undoubtedly this form of restrictive immigration policy helped to reduce unemployment.
37. In the United Kingdom, for example, the unemployment rate among unskilled manual workers in 1980 was 16.7% compared with 6.7% among skilled manual and 2.3% among professional workers. See Micklewright (1984: 42). The regional unemployment rate was 17.3% in North England compared to 9.5% in South-East England. Unemployment among black and Asian workers was twice that of all workers, with even greater inequality among teenage unemployed. See Moon and Richardson (1985: 28–9).
38. OECD (1980: 43).
39. See, for example, 'Sweden's economy', *The Economist* (7 March 1987).

40.    Panitch (1986: 112).
41.    Panitch (1986: 112).
42.    Korpi (1983: 20–1).
43.    Stephens (1979: 122–3); Banting (1986: 5–7); Rothstein (1987).
44.    See Albage (1986: 113–16; 119–20); Fjällström (1986: 119–20);
       'Sweden's economy', *The Economist* (7 March 1987); Panitch (1986:
       61–3).
45.    Luther (1987: 377–8, 383–5, 393–6); OECD (1988d: 30).
46.    Albage (1986); 'Sweden's economy', *The Economist* (7 March 1987);
       Panitch (1986: 61–3).
47.    Fjällström (1986: 121).
48.    Fjällström (1986: 121).
49.    In 1970, 1.8% of the labour force was in these programmes and 1.3%
       of GDP was spent on labour-market policies. In 1984 the correspond-
       ing figures were 4.1% and 3.0%, respectively. See Jangenas (1985:
       16–17).
50.    'Sweden's economy', *The Economist* (7 March 1987). According to a
       recent study of 18 OECD countries, Sweden had the most flexible
       labour market in its ability to respond to sudden economic and
       technological changes. A Brookings Institution study found that
       labour mobility (changing jobs) in Sweden was as high as that in the
       United States.
51.    See, for example, Myles (1988: 92–3, 98–100).
52.    Olsson (1987: 96).
53.    Hagemann *et al.* (1988: 208); OECD (1985a: 58–9); Walters (1985:
       365–7). See also note 28 above.
54.    Olsson (1987: 94–7); Marklund (1988: 78–80).
55.    Olsson (1987: 94).
56.    Olsson (1987: 98).
57.    In 1987 Austria ranked eighth among 23 OECD countries in respect
       of taxes as a proportion of GDP (42%) and thirteenth in respect of
       income taxes as a proportion of GDP. See OECD (1987–8: 33).
58.    Luther (1987: 383–4).
59.    Luther (1987: 380–1, 386, 392–3).
60.    Luther (1987: 393, 396); OECD (1988a: 30).
61.    See, for example, Esping-Andersen (1985); and Harding (1989).

# 4

# Social policy and the new models: Canada and Australia

This chapter looks at the diffusion of neo-conservatism beyond the 'classic' cases of the United Kingdom and the United States and that of social corporatism beyond Scandinavia and Austria. It examines the experience of two countries in particular, Canada and Australia. In 1984 a Progressive Conservative (Tory) government swept to power in Canada with a landslide victory and a mandate for change. The victory of the Conservatives came at a time when Canada's southern neighbour was in the full flush of Reaganomics. President Reagan was soon to win a second term of office, also by a landslide. These circumstances presaged the possibility of a right turn also in Canada. Meanwhile, Australia was moving in the opposite direction. In 1983 a Labour government took office in Australia on the basis of a prices and incomes agreement – 'the Accord' – with trade unions. Among other things, it was expected that the Accord would enable the government to improve the social wage and rebuild the welfare state after its attrition during the previous eight years under Conservative governments. In brief, these two predominantly English-speaking countries[1] seemed poised for a new departure in social policy. At the time of writing (1989) both these governments remain in office. How far has Canada followed the path of neo-conservatism – in short, the strategy of retrenching the welfare state? Conversely, how far has Australia practised social corporatism as a strategy for rebuilding and maintaining the welfare state? And finally, does the experience of these two countries support our arguments about these policy models in their classical locale? This chapter is an attempt to answer these questions.

## Canada

Federal politics in Canada has not witnessed strong policy differences between the two major national parties – the Liberals and
Conservatives. Both parties have practised a form of 'brokerage
politics' – a pragmatic, non-ideological consensus politics of the
centre. The 1984 election was no exception to this rule.[2] Although
'change' was a basic theme in the election, this change was
essentially about the process of government and the *style* of
leadership rather than the substance of economic and social policy.[3]
Although Conservatives voiced concern about the budget deficit
and promised to reduce it, at the same time they also promised to
maintain social programmes and social expenditure – indeed they
proposed improvements and additions.[4] Government intervention
in the economy was to be curtailed but this referred to privatization
of nationalized undertakings (so-called 'Crown corporations') and
the deregulation of business and economic life rather than to social
policies and expenditures.[5] Put simply, the Conservatives, who
have chiefly been in opposition rather than in government in
Canada, were rooting for victory at the polls. Hence a centrist social
policy platform which represented the broad consensus of opinion
over social welfare in Canada seemed the safe course and indeed
was followed by Conservatives.[6] It was only after winning the
election and forming the government that they began to sing a
different tune.

Once in office the Conservative government unveiled an agenda
which included a thorough review of social policies and programmes. Reducing the budget deficit now emerged as a top
priority. It was seen as critical for restoring private confidence and
business investment – the key to economic renewal and growth.
Hence public expenditure in general and social expenditure in
particular were singled out for reduction. Universality of social
programmes with the exception of medical care was no longer to be
regarded as sacrosanct. Rather, the government put forward 'social
responsibility', defined as directing 'scarce resources to those in
greatest need' (a euphemism for selectivity), as the guiding
principle. Selectivity was seen as a way of reducing programme
expenditures equitably and also as a way of increasing the effectiveness of social programmes through targeting those in greatest need.
These reform proposals were put forward as part of a wider agenda

for change.[7] Within days of taking office, the government appointed a Task Force chaired by Erik Nielsen to review federal social programmes (about a thousand of them). Unemployment insurance (UI), however, was considered important enough to be the subject of a special commission of inquiry.[8] It was felt, among other things, that UI restricted labour mobility and contributed towards unemployment. Overall, the new government's rhetoric and plans were grandiose, suggesting a major initiative in reducing the size of the public sector in social welfare and in breaking with the principle of universality. These moves, seen in conjunction with expenditure cuts announced shortly after the Conservatives took office with the promise of further cuts to come, seemed to set the scene for the unfolding of a neo-conservative style agenda.[9] However, the next year and a half were to see a retreat from the assault on such basic principles of the welfare state as universality as well as a retreat from attempted cutbacks in universal programmes such as old-age pensions.[10] The following pages review Conservative policy with respect to the three major components of the welfare state: full employment; universal social programmes; and the maintenance of a basic minimum, that is, anti-poverty measures.

## Full employment

Unlike Britain, Canada did not pursue a policy of full employment in the post-war years. In this respect it has emulated the United States rather than Western Europe. As a result, the Canadian rate of unemployment in the post-war years has been similar to that of the United States and a good deal higher than those in Western Europe.[11]

During the 1960s unemployment in Canada hovered around 5.0%. It rose gradually in the following decade, averaging more than 7.0% in the late 1970s. As the Canadian economy went into recession in 1982 on the back of a world recession, unemployment climbed to double digits and stayed there for the next three years (see Table 1, Appendix 2). The country was just beginning to recover from its worst post-war recession with an unemployment rate of 10.5% and an inflation rate of 4.5% when the Conservatives came to power. Monetarism in the form of high interest rates was already being practised by the outgoing Liberal government.[12]

Unemployment was at a record high, while inflation had been reduced substantially. There was, therefore, little scope for a neo-conservative deflationary policy of high interest rates which would drive unemployment up still further, exert a downward pressure on wages and bring down inflation. Such policies had already been practised by Liberal governments in the 1970s. Rather, unemployment was *the* major concern of Canadians in 1984 and the Conservative promise of 'jobs, jobs and jobs' through the classic approach of private-sector-led growth reflected this. Growth was to be promoted through deregulation, the reduction of the budget deficit and by other means of creating a climate favourable to private enterprise.[13]

In the event, as the Canadian economy began to pull out of the recession, unemployment started coming down. This process has continued and probably owes little to Conservative policy. The main point to note is that Canadian governments, unlike those in Western European countries such as Britain, West Germany, Sweden and Austria, have never assumed responsibility for maintaining full employment. There was, therefore, no need for a neo-conservative ideology which would repudiate the state's role in maintaining employment. In this sense Canada has been neo-conservative for a long time.

However, more than its predecessors, the Mulroney government has expressed concern about unemployment benefits both as a drain on public resources and as a major source of economic, especially labour, rigidity. The belief that UI benefits stood in the way of labour mobility and industrial adaptation has influenced the Mulroney government's thinking rather more than that of its Liberal predecessors. Although restrictions placed on UI benefits by the Conservatives have not been very different from those imposed by Liberal governments since the mid-1970s, it must be remembered that the Commission of Inquiry appointed by the government was expected to recommend major changes.[14] Reporting in 1986, the Forget Commission did in fact recommend substantial changes. Most of these were in line with the principle of restricting benefits in order to discourage both labour and capital from being locked into regions which were low-wage and declining economically. 'Restructuring' of UI benefits as a form of rationalization rather than downright reduction was the main theme of the Commission's report. However, the Commission was divided and a minority (the Labour members) produced a separate report. In the event the government decided not to implement the Commission's recommendations.[15]

Meanwhile, unemployment has continued to decline slowly. At just under 8%, it is still high even by Canadian post-war standards. The proportion of long-term unemployed (that is, those out of work for six months or more) increased from 16.8% in 1980 to 27.6% in 1985 but has declined somewhat recently.[16] Over the years the unemployed, and in particular the long-term unemployed, have had to resort increasingly to social assistance (welfare) and more recently to charities and food banks.[17]

## Universal social services

As we noted earlier, the Conservative election campaign pledged to maintain universal social programmes. Indeed, far from *reducing* social expenditures, the Conservatives proposed to improve some of the benefits and to provide new services in the area of pre-school child care (day care).[18] Once in office, however, they began to express serious concern about the size of the budget deficit. The government claimed that the real deficit was a good deal higher than was earlier believed on the basis of the previous government's calculations.[19] The implications were clear. Spending had to be further restrained. The Conservatives were not keen to consider the alternative of increased taxation, even though studies had shown clearly that one of the main reasons for the deficit was a serious drop in revenue. Revenue loss in turn was a result of the indexation of tax brackets and allowances since the early 1970s, the granting of various tax allowances and concessions during the 1970s and early 1980s, and the practice of tax avoidance by many large corporations.[20] As might be expected, the Conservative strategy was to reduce public expenditure rather than to increase revenue. Again, this was not new. Liberal governments had been practising 're-straint' for years. What was new and different –at least symbolically – was the proposal to break with the principle of universality.

The government's major statement on economic and social policy called for 'a frank and open discussion' about social programmes.[21] It proposed widespread consultation and debate on ways of restructuring income-maintenance programmes, that is, making programmes such as family allowance and age pensions more selective. The guiding principle was to be 'social responsibility', that is, that 'scarce resources should be diverted first to those in greatest need'.[22] During the election campaign the principle of universality had been declared a 'sacred trust not to be tampered with'.[23] The 'sacred trust' now began to be seen as a 'sacred cow'. The Prime Minister now saw it as a question on which he was 'open to dialogue and consultation'. More specifically, he asked: 'Are we making proper use of taxpayers' money by giving a bank president who makes $500,000 or $600,000 a year a baby bonus [family allowance]? Should that money not be more properly used to assist someone who desperately needs help?'[24]

The fear voiced earlier by critics that the Conservatives had a 'hidden agenda' now seemed justified. The proposal to break with universality led to a nationwide outcry. It was seen as a clear breach of trust with the electorate, especially in light of the Conservative leader's solemn undertaking that universality was a sacred trust. The furore over the issue prompted a retreat and by early 1985 the government had repudiated the idea of means-testing and other forms of departure from universality on these income-maintenance programmes.[25]

The second round in the attempt to restrain spending on universal programmes began in the middle of 1985. The government proposed to deindex old-age pensions and family allowances by 3% (that is to say, payments were to be increased only by the amount of inflation in excess of 3%). Personal income taxes were also to be deindexed. *Pari passu* with these measures, the government was planning to give major tax breaks to the rich while imposing a greater tax burden on lower- and middle-income groups.[26] Public reaction to deindexing of benefits was strong. 'The issue became the focal point for all the grievance and complaints about the budget itself and seemed to offer the greatest proof to the government's detractors that the Tories were the party of the rich and privileged.'[27]

Such was the protest and outcry on pensions that the government beat a hasty retreat. Deindexing of family allowances, on the other hand, did not evoke a comparable protest. It went ahead as planned.[28]

By mid-1986, two years after the Conservatives had come to office, the zeal for radical change and reform had cooled considerably. Instead of reducing the deficit by cutting social expenditures, the government now planned to increase taxes.[29] These new tax arrangements were on the whole regressive, but compared with similar developments in the United States and in Britain they were modest in their scope for upward redistribution of income.[30] In early 1986 the Nielsen Task Force (see page 71 above) released its report. The expectation that it might recommend *substantial* cuts in social programmes and their privatization was not fulfilled. For example, the Task Force did not find expenditure on the Canada Assistance Plan, the major social assistance programme 'excessive relative to its purpose', nor could it find 'support for any major alternative to the Canada Assistance Plan (CAP) in terms of social policy'.[31] A commentator on its interim report observed that, paralleling the cases of universality and deindexation of pensions, it, too, bore 'many footprints of political retreat', and that, far from building a head of steam for major changes, 'for now it must be considered a fizzle'.[32] This could easily stand as the judgment on its final report at least as far as the retrenchment of government programmes was concerned.[33] We have already noted the government's decision not to act on the recommendations of the Forget Commission's report to restructure UI (see page 73 above). By the end of 1986 it was clear that the government had abandoned its half-hearted attempt to break with the centrist consensus in Canada over social protection.

## Poverty and the basic minimum

With unemployment rising in the 1980s, especially by three full percentage points in the recession of 1982, the incidence of poverty in Canada rose sharply. The proportion of population in poverty increased from 14.7% in 1981 to 16.1% in 1982, 17.1% in 1983 and 17.3% in 1984.[34] Hardship was felt by an increasing number of Canadians – prominent among them the unemployed and their families – who were forced to turn to social assistance.[35] Unlike Britain, social assistance in Canada is under provincial and municipal jurisdiction. Rates vary across provinces and on average provide something like one-half to two-thirds of the level of poverty income to welfare recipients.[36] Given the gross inadequacy of welfare payments and the increase in the numbers of unemployed and single-parent families, hunger has surfaced as a social problem for those in need. Many have to resort to food banks and other charities which have stepped in to fill the gap left by grossly inadequate as well as stigmatizing social assistance.[37]

Not surprisingly perhaps, the Nielsen Task Force, 'which was widely expected to recommend drastic changes to Canada's welfare system, instead called for the maintaining and strengthening of CAP, albeit with some warnings about the budgetary dangers to the program'.[38]

Overall, then, it is fair to conclude that, in sharp contrast to the United States, Conservatives in Canada have not so far attempted to retrench means-tested and other selective programmes which constitute a 'safety net', however weak and threadbare.[39] None the less, the combined effect of the Conservative policy on taxation and expenditure cuts has been in the direction of greater inequality of incomes and living standards, although this has been mitigated somewhat by the fall in unemployment.[40] However, the point is that as far as equality, social protection and the safety net are concerned a good deal of erosion can take place through default rather than design. In this respect Conservatives may be said to have continued the policies of the recent past. Thus far, however, changes have been somewhat modest compared to those in the United States and Britain.[41]

### Conclusions

The Conservative government which came to power in Canada in 1984 did not seek or have a mandate to break the centrist mould of Canadian social policy. Neither the Conservatives' pronouncements nor their rhetoric on social policy suggested a radical change of course. Indeed their leader's assurance that universality of social programmes would be fully respected implied the acceptance of the broad parameters of Canadian social policy. Yet upon assuming office the new government did try to move in a neo-conservative direction, notably in its attempt to break with universality in income-maintenance programmes to reduce social expenditure substantially. If this seemed like a 'breach of trust' with the electorate it was by no means unique to the federal Conservatives. Right-wing governments at the provincial level in Canada, notably in British Columbia, show a similar pattern.[42] In Britain, too, Thatcherite Conservatives, the first neo-conservative government in the West, not only did not propose cuts in social programmes and expenditures in 1979 but repeatedly denied that proposed tax reductions would in any way affect social expenditures. It was only some time after winning office that Thatcherite Conservatives began to consider substantial privatization and retrenchment of the welfare state. They, too, backpedalled rather smartly when there was a nation-wide outcry about a hidden agenda of dismantling social programmes (see page 23 above). The Canadian experience seems to confirm the judgment that the heartland of the welfare state – universal social programmes which serve the broad majority of the population – remains popular and that no party can hope to win elections on a platform which proposes their retrenchment. Neo-conservatives therefore try to retrench social welfare services *after* being elected to office. However, as both Reagan and Thatcher governments demonstrate, it is difficult politically to retrench mainstream programmes – at least directly. The axe therefore tends to fall on unpopular minority programmes such as general welfare assistance and low-income housing. This is accompanied by a gradualist strategy of underfunding mainstream programmes, such as pensions and health care, and encouraging their private provision. The ideology of individual responsibility and self-reliance also legitimizes government withdrawal from the responsibility for maintaining minimum incomes and preventing poverty. Moreover, since voluntarism is extolled, charitable and philanthropic assistance is seen as stepping in as government steps out of social welfare. The Canadian government has not *so far* moved towards this brand of neo-conservatism, at least as policy. There has been no *deliberate* move to retrench services for the poor (for example, the Canada Assistance Plan and social housing) in the manner of the United States under Reagan. In this sense Canadian neo-conservatism has not so far followed in the footsteps of the United States and Britain.

In yet another respect the Conservative approach in Canada has differed from that in the United Kingdom and the United States. Conservatives won the election in part on the promise of a new *style* of government. It was to be governance through consultation and national reconciliation (a reference to federal–provincial relations and to the ever sensitive regional issues) in contrast with the

centralized and high-handed approach of previous Liberal governments. Indeed, national reconciliation and a consensus-building
approach were an important part of the Conservative platform.
True to their word, the Conservatives did put in place a fairly wide
consultative process in which policy changes proposed by the
government were widely discussed and debated before making a
decision. This commitment to consultation and reconciliation of
differences among Canadians has been an important feature of the
Mulroney government which sets it apart from the ideological,
hardline and confrontational style of government of both Thatcher
and Reagan. This commitment has been more than symbolic. It has
helped prevent unpopular policies from being sprung on the nation
and bulldozed through the legislature at a time when Conservatives
had a commanding majority.[43]

To sum up: as far as social policy is concerned the Mulroney
government did not begin its career as a neo-conservative government. In so far as it did move in that direction it was forced to
retrace its steps towards the centrist consensus prevalent in Canada.
This judgment does not conflict with the observation that the
government's strategy has been 'to shift federal policies and
expenditures in a right-wing small-c conservative direction'. As the
same commentator remarks: 'Tory measures on pension reform,
training programs, regulatory reforms and restraint of social
programs are not radically different from previous Liberal governments.'[44] It is in fields other than social welfare – notably free trade
with the United States, privatization of Crown corporations and the
dismantling of the National Energy Program – that the Conservative agenda has differed substantially from that of the former
Liberal government.[45]

Clearly, both the neo-conservative agenda and its implementation have to be understood within the context of a nation's political
history and institutions. In Canada electoral considerations emerge
as a particularly important constraint on a Progressive Conservative
Party whose political life has largely been spent on opposition
benches and which, unlike Conservatives in Britain, cannot assume
a weak and ineffectual political opposition. Again, Canada differs
from the United States under Reagan with respect to both
ideological consensus around social welfare and the institutional
context of politics. The idea that policy development in the United
States tends to be episodic ('big bang') and in Canada continuous

('steady-state') seems also to be true of the political economy of welfare state retrenchment.[46] In the absence of an unexpected external or internal shock to the system, social developments in Canada are likely to remain centrist and evolutionary. None the less, continuing restraint and piecemeal retrenchment can cumulatively weaken the fabric of the welfare state (see also page 99 below on the free trade agreement with the United States and its implications).

## Australia

Post-war Australia has been ruled chiefly by Conservative governments. Between 1949 and 1983 the Labour Party held office for only three years, from 1972 to 1975, under Gough Whitlam. Though short-lived, the Whitlam government set in motion an impressive programme for the development and modernization of the Australian welfare state. And there was a great deal to be done.

Like Britain but unlike Canada and the United States, Australia had a full-employment economy until the early 1970s. However, the situation was very different with respect to social welfare services. Instead of a social insurance programme for income maintenance, Australia, along with New Zealand, had developed a system of means-tested (in the broader sense of the term) categoric programmes such as old-age pensions and unemployment benefits. There was only one universal benefit – family allowances. There was no general scheme of medical care.[47]

The Whitlam government had plans for a major expansion and reform of the social welfare system. These included abolishing the means-testing of old-age pensions and other income-maintenance programmes and developing a national superannuation scheme. It succeeded in establishing a national health-care programme (Medibank) as well as the Australian Assistance Plan (AAP), a programme of federal (Commonwealth) support for establishing in-kind social services at the local level.[48] Medibank and the AAP were virtually dismantled by the Conservative Fraser government during its eight-year rule (1975–83) which succeeded the Whitlam government. More generally, the Fraser government followed a right-wing policy which favoured withdrawing government from social welfare and encouraging private and market-based provision.[49] Meanwhile, unemployment continued to rise, edging close to 10% by 1983 (see Table 1, Appendix 2).

It is against such a background that a Labour government led by Bob Hawke came to power in 1983. A social contract (that is, a prices and incomes accord with the trade-union movement) was the central plank in the Labour Party platform. The Accord was based on the principle of wage restraint on the part of trade unions in order to contain inflation and a corresponding expansionary monetary and fiscal policy to be followed by the government so as to revive growth, reduce unemployment and improve the social wage. A general approach to economic governance through consensus and reconciliation and through tripartite consultation between trade unions, employers and the state was to be a distinctive feature of the new government.[50]

It is significant that the labour movement in Australia chose the path of social contract and tripartism. A prices and incomes accord was without precedent in that country. In the United Kingdom, the only English-speaking country where a social contract had recently been tried, it had ended in a dismal failure. Why, then, did the Australian Labour Party embark on it? Clearly, in the economic and political circumstances of the 1980s tripartism appeared to be one of the major strategies available to the labour movement in its attempt to reconcile the twin objectives of economic growth and social justice.

The Accord between the Australian trade-union movement and the government has been sustained since Labour came to power in 1983, having since won three successive elections. What has the Accord achieved? To what extent has the government tried to maintain – or, more accurately, build – the Australian welfare state, since it was not well developed in any case and was scaled down very considerably during the Fraser years? Finally, what lessons can be learned from Australia's experiment with the Accord with respect to its potential for sustaining the welfare state? The rest of this chapter is an attempt to answer these questions.

### Full employment

Until the early 1970s Australia enjoyed full employment. Unemployment averaged 1.9% during 1960–7 and 2.0% during

1968–73 but rose to an average of 5.0% during 1974–9. Between 1980 and 1982 it averaged 6.3% (see Tables 1 and 6, Appendix 2).

A combination of recession and drought took unemployment close to double digits in 1983. Meanwhile, inflation was running at over 10% and the economy was stagnating with a growth rate close to zero in 1982 and 1983 (see Table 2, Appendix 2). In 1984, thanks to the expansionary fiscal and monetary policy followed by the new Labour government, the economy posted a growth of 6.7%, while the prices and incomes policy based on the Accord brought inflation down to 3.9%. Unemployment, however, fell by only one percentage point (from 9.9% to 8.9%). Subsequently economic growth was sustained but with little difference in unemployment (see Tables 1 and 2, Appendix 2). The latter stood at 8.1% in 1987, a good deal higher than in the late 1970s and early 1980s.[51]

Not surprisingly, long-term unemployment has increased, with the average duration of unemployment at 49.5 weeks in 1985, compared with 17.5 weeks in 1976.[52] While the government has taken some steps to alleviate unemployment, overall the policy is to rely on the private sector for job creation while facilitating growth through macroeconomic management of the economy.[53]

Clearly, the government cannot be said to have moved far towards reducing unemployment, not to say restoring full employment. Moreover, current debates around the Accord and its social policy leave one with the impression that reduction of unemployment is not a high priority for the partners of the Accord, nor for that matter for the social welfare constituency generally. We shall return to this question later in this chapter.

### Universal social services

As noted above, unlike most Western industrial countries, Australia does not have a system of universal social security programmes. Furthermore, it was also noted that the Conservative government which was in power during 1975–83 virtually dismantled two of the major initiatives of its predecessor: Medibank and the Australia Assistance Plan. It scaled down substantially not only the social programmes of the Whitlam years but also others put in place by earlier Conservative governments. The Fraser years, in short, saw a major retreat from the welfare state.[54] To what extent has the Hawke government tried to reverse the process and with what consequences? In what other ways has it sought to develop the welfare state?

The social policy platform of the Australian Labour Party in 1983 included the restoration of Medibank. This was done under the new title of Medicare.[55] With respect to income security, however, the Hawke government has followed a cautious policy of improving benefits somewhat for the disadvantaged rather than moving towards universality. Old-age pensions have been increased but fall short of the level of 25% of average male earnings promised by the government. During the Whitlam years there was a clear intention to move towards universality in income maintenance programmes. This has not been the case with the Hawke government.[56] In 1984 the government reinstated the assets test for old-age pensions.[57] While this could be seen as a step towards achieving greater equity within the present framework of means-tested benefits, it has done nothing to move the system in a universal direction. Indeed the government is considering the regulation and extension of occupational superannuation as the basis for retirement pensions.[58] Overall, the income-support strategy of the government seems to be one of alleviating poverty rather than of developing a comprehensive social welfare system based on the principle of universal social insurance. Selectivity and targeting those in greatest need have become the centre-piece of government social policy. This has been particularly evident since 1985, when the Australian economy ran into serious difficulties. Thus the only universal income-security benefit, family allowances, became subject to an income test in December 1986.[59] In recent years concern with the size of the budget deficit and its reduction has become more prominent, so much so that 'current debates revolve not around whether expenditure cutbacks should take place but how large they should be and what form they should take'.[60] Concern with reducing the deficit and the 'political imperative not to increase taxes has in turn translated into the perceived need to cut government expenditure'.[61] The latter, naturally enough, has meant the reduction of social expenditure and, in particular, expenditure on social security. Fiscal restraint and selectivity seem, therefore, to have emerged as general policy guidelines in social welfare since early 1985. Commonwealth (federal) budget outlays declined in the fiscal year 1983–4 from 29.6% of GDP to 26.6% of GDP in 1987–8.[62] Reductions have affected a wide range of programmes, 'with the largest cuts in health and social security, education, defense and foreign aid' in the 1986–7 budget.[63] Through a combination of higher revenues by means of changes in taxation, and lower expenditures, the federal budget deficit as a percentage of GDP was cut by half between 1985–6 and 1986–7.[64] The government seems to have responded eagerly to the clamour to reduce social expenditure. It seems to have paid little regard to the fact that, with the tradition of a selective income-security system, Australia has one of the lowest levels of social spending among OECD countries.[65] Yet tax expenditures are substantial. According to recent estimates, tax expenditures connected with superannuation amount to 46% of the outlays on old-age pensions and allowances.[66]

True, taxation has been an important component of the general policy issues with which the Accord has been concerned. Following the Tax Summit of 1985, the government took steps to make taxation more equitable and to reduce income taxes as a trade-off against the reduction in wages. Lump-sum superannuation payments, fringe benefits and capital gains became taxable while the top income-tax rate was reduced from 60% to 55%, with a further drop projected to 49%.[67] Various measures to curb tax evasion have also formed a part of this tax reform. However, income taxes remain the principal source of government revenue out of which social security and other social welfare programmes (apart from medical care, for which there is an earmarked levy) are largely financed. Since Australia does not have a social insurance scheme, there are no social security or payroll taxes to finance income-maintenance and health-care programmes. Therefore, although Australia remains a low-tax country with respect to taxation as a whole, personal income is heavily taxed (see Table 7, Appendix 2).[68] Under these circumstances the prospect of developing and sustaining universal social programmes depends in part on the government's ability to raise revenue from sources less visible than the personal income tax. However, the government is more committed to reducing income taxes than to building a network of universal services.[69] In the absence of universal benefits there is keen resentment against means-tested income security payments financed out of income taxes. The tax–welfare backlash is strong and seems to be getting stronger.[70] Meanwhile, the government has instituted a major review of social security. What principles the review will enunciate for Australian social security and how the government will respond to its recommendations remains to be seen.[71]

### Poverty and a basic minimum

Full employment and a set of universal social services may be said to constitute the major line of defence against poverty. Social assistance and other special provisions for needs not adequately met by universal social services form the second line of defence – in short, the social safety net.

As we have seen, Australia now not only falls far short of the level of full employment, it also lacks an important ingredient of the welfare state – *universal* income-maintenance programmes. Given the country's tradition of means-tested income support pro-grammes, the emphasis of the Hawke government and the Austra-lian trade-union movement has been and continues to be on the alleviation of poverty. But how adequate are the social assistance programmes? More important, how far has government policy, including the Accord, been helpful in achieving anti-poverty objectives?

The Australian government does not seem to conduct a regular survey of the low-income population. It is difficult, therefore, to estimate recent changes in poverty.[72] However, given that benefits paid under the Australian income-security system tend to be flat-rate and rather modest, they are not very effective in alleviating poverty. It is estimated, for example, that in 1981–2 over 15% of those receiving old-age pensions, 42% of those receiving supporting parents' benefits and 50% of those receiving unemployment benefits had an income below the poverty line.[73] Indeed, poverty figures for families tend to rise dramatically with duration of unemployment. From a mere 6% for those fully employed, the percentage rises to nearly 50% for those unemployed for over six months and to 65% for those unemployed for over a year.[74] There can be little doubt that with unemployment now lasting on an average nearly a year (see page 81 above) poverty and hardship are likely to be widespread among the unemployed. Persistent high unemployment is also likely to affect other dependent groups adversely. In the context of unemployment, changing demographic and other social trends such as more single-parent households, also mean increasing poverty.[75]

The Labour government has taken some steps to help alleviate poverty. For example, a family income supplement was introduced in 1983 while income-tested children's allowances have been increased substantially since 1983. But, as Cass remarks, these allowances are not indexed. Despite substantial increases, therefore, their real value remains below the level of the mid-1970s chiefly because they were allowed to decline for a long period of time.[76] Old-age pensions, sickness and unemployment benefits were also lower in real value in 1985–6 than a decade earlier chiefly because various additional allowances have not been indexed.[77]

The social security review mentioned already (see page 84 above) is examining the problem of poverty and the adequacy of income-maintenance programmes and is expected to recommend a substantial restructuring of the present system. However, as we noted above, the government seems to be wedded to the idea of a selective approach. Selectivity has a strong appeal both on fiscal grounds and on grounds of helping those who need help the most. In Australia it is likely to be stronger in view of traditional reliance on social assistance and the absence of universal programmes. But, as Saunders remarks:

> Greater reliance on universalist principles may be an unpopular proposition in the current Australian context. But the fact that those countries which had adopted this approach are characterized by both more redistribution and less income inequality should at the very least lead to some serious questioning of the merits of the selectivist approach.[78]

So far there is little evidence that the government or Accord partners are beginning to appreciate the critical role of universal social services in reducing inequality and preventing poverty.

## Conclusions

In 1983 a Labour government came to power in Australia on the basis of a prices and incomes accord with the organized trade-union movement. While the unions agreed on wage restraint by way of indexation, the government sought to build a tripartite if not a broader consensus around major economic and social objectives. Prominent among these were promoting economic growth, strengthening the nation's economy, improving the social wage and creating a more equitable society. When the Hawke government took office both unemployment and inflation were in double digits and the economy was stagnating. Social expenditure had been reduced substantially during the period of the Fraser government and major social initiatives of the Whitlam era, such as Medibank, had been turned back. Thus the Hawke government faced the task not so much of maintaining as of strengthening and building an underdeveloped welfare state which had been weakened considerably during the previous eight years of Conservative rule.

In 1985 Australia's economic situation deteriorated mainly because of international factors. The result was a large balance-of-payments deficit, a rise in inflation, a stagnating economy and a plummeting Australian dollar. The government responded with a tighter monetary and fiscal policy. Beginning in May 1985 successive budgets reduced social expenditure substantially and the government accepted the principle of selectivity at least as far as income maintenance was concerned. The so-called 'trilogy' – a commitment not to let taxation, public expenditure or the budget deficit rise as a proportion of GDP during the lifetime of the last parliament – made social expenditure cuts and selectivity almost inevitable. A government that is obsessively concerned with the budget deficit, which seeks to restrain social expenditure, accepts the traditional selectivity of Australia's income-security programmes and which lives with an unemployment rate of 8% can scarcely claim to be engaged in building and restoring the welfare state. Indeed, not only does unemployment remain high, and not only is social welfare under restraint, but also, as a result of voluntary wage restraint, workers have suffered a drop in wages. Between 1984 and 1987 real average earnings declined by 4.5%.[79] It is significant that the Accord has not broken down. Since 1987 the unions have agreed to a two-tier incomes policy which allows greater flexibility in wage determination, for example in relation to productivity. Clearly, unions still see the Accord in a positive light and hope to be able to influence government economic and industrial policy in favour of wage-earners in the long run. Moreover, the unions undoubtedly consider the present government preferable to its alternative: Conservative rule. Thanks largely to the Accord, the Labour government has won three successive elections, a remarkable victory not only in the Australian political context but also in the context of the international politics of the 1980s. No doubt, judged against the hardline Conservative politics of the Fraser government and in light of the problems which beset the reforming Whitlam Labour government in the mid-1970s, the modest social democracy of the Hawke government appears more acceptable than it otherwise might. Since the government took office at least unemployment has been reduced and held down, inflation has been kept under control, wage indexation has allowed wages to move broadly in line with prices and a system of medical care has been put in place. Given wage restraint, it has been easier to control inflation, reflate the economy and generate growth. Furthermore, taxation policy has been addressed within the wider context of economic and social policy objectives – efficiency, equity and revenue consideraitons. Clearly, the compartmentalization of economic, fiscal, industrial and social policies – a hallmark of the 'differentiated welfare state' of the Keynes–Beveridge variety – has been overcome within a system of 'trade-offs' between various national objectives.[80] The Accord has made possible both an incomes policy and an orderly system of industrial relations. That, in turn, has enabled the Labour government to remain in office with the promise of doing more towards the development of an effective economic (including industrial) and social policy. Through the Accord the union movement has been able to move beyond its status as an economic interest group, representing particular sections of workers and engaged in collective bargaining with employers on their behalf, to a broader societal movement seeking to influence the economic and social development of the country so that it might favour the interests of the non-propertied masses. The economic modernization of the Australian economy is among the objectives being pursued by the Labour government in recognition that in the long run the social wage depends on economic growth.

However, experience since 1984 has made a number of things quite clear. First, the phenomenon of 'workless growth' means that economic growth as such cannot generate enough jobs to mop up unemployment. More substantive government intervention may be necessary. Second, given the legacy of a distinctive pattern of income maintenance based on selectivity, a move towards universality requires a major social policy initiative. Third, given the financial, ideological and economic climate of the 1980s such developments seem unlikely.

Overall, then, Australia's experiment with a 'social contract' and the latter's survival since 1983 in a country which has never had a voluntary incomes policy, suggests a number of things. First, it underlines the relevance of social corporatism. The latter is *not* an exotic plant peculiar to Scandinavia and central Europe. The failure of the Social Contract in Britain in the 1970s does not mean that English-speaking countries cannot develop an institutional framework for reconciling economic and social policies around a set of national objectives. On the other hand, the modest achievements of the Hawke government with regard to the welfare state show that its commitment to social justice and welfare remains somewhat circumscribed. In this respect the Hawke government's policy falls far short of the stronger welfare state orientation of countries such as Sweden and Austria. It has lacked the commitment to restore full employment and to develop a universal income maintenance system. Worse, its approach to deficit reduction via social expenditure cutbacks is more akin to neo-conservatism than to social corporatism.

Australia thus shows that the social contract, with its underlying integrative approach, is largely a *form* – an institutional arrangement for managing the mixed economy of welfare capitalism. It has the *potential* for combining economic growth with social justice. But the *content* of policies followed under a social contract is not entailed by the form and depends on wider societal factors. It seems that factors conducive to a strong pro-labour policy within social corporatism have not been present in Australia.[81] At the very least, however, the Accord has made it possible to halt or at least slow down the slide towards a dual society and dual economy that seemed to have been well under way during the Fraser years. As one commentator candidly remarks: 'Prospects for a fairer Australia certainly rest, at a minimum, on keeping the New Right out of policy implementation.'[82] He might have added that the latter is a necessary but not a sufficient condition. No doubt the Australian experience confirms what critics of tripartism and social contract have argued often enough – that it is no panacea, no short-cut to the full-employment universal citizenship welfare state. In Australia, moreover, the government has had to face a situation rather different from that of countries such as Sweden and Austria. It has not been concerned primarily with defending a well-constructed welfare state put in place in happier times. Rather, it has been faced with the task of building a full-employment universal welfare state in a country with a legacy of a selectivist income-maintenance policy and a high marginal rate of income tax. Not surprisingly, the *building* of a welfare state in the economic, financial and political context of the 1980s is a more arduous undertaking than that of *defending* a structure already in place.

Finally, we must examine one other argument. It is the charge that the:

> effect of government's policies is to benefit those involved in relations of production at the expense of those who are excluded from them. The Accord has marginalised the poor, the unemployed, the single parents and other welfare dependents who . . . have nowhere else to take their votes.[83]

Earlier we discussed this question in a general way and specifically in relation to Sweden and Austria. Do the same arguments apply here or has the Australian experience been different?

We argued earlier (see Chapter 3) that there is little validity for the assumption that a social contract and tripartism constitute an open conspiracy by organized producer interests against the rest of society. If, instead of arguing from a priori assumptions, we examine the objectives and consequences of the social contract, it is hard to find any validity for the above assertion. Take, for example, the objectives of wage restraint, the containment of inflation and economic growth. Of these, the first is more likely to work in favour of equity and fairness in wages rather than an increase in the share of wages *per se* in income distribution. There is even less justification for suggesting that price stability favours producer interests. Economic growth, for its part, may be considered neutral. Turning to the social wage, can we say that the restoration of medical care, perhaps the major social welfare measure of the Hawke government, is in favour of producer interests? Furthermore, during 1985–7 real wages declined by about 2.5% annually – a datum that hardly supports the theory of producer bias. Rather, reductions in economic wages have paralleled those in social expenditure, thus requiring wage-earners to share in austerity measures.[84] It should also be noted that social

**Table 4.1**   Commonwealth of Australia budget outlays (percentage change over the period at constant prices)

|  | Between 1975–6 and 1982–3 | Between 1982–3 and 1985–6 |
|---|---|---|
| Education | −0.6 | 3.5 |
| Health | −43.0 | 57.3 |
| Social Security and Welfare | 37.0* | 6.6 |
| Housing and Community Development | −60.0 | 45.9 |
| Culture and Recreation | 4.1 | 32.5 |
| Total social expenditure | 0.2 | 15.7 |

*Mainly accounted for by unemployment benefit payments.

*Source*: Jamrozik (1987: 62).

**Table 4.2**   Rate of social security payments in Australia (annual percentage change at constant prices)

|  | From 1975–6 to 1982–3 | From 1982–3 to 1984–5 |
|---|---|---|
| Age and service pensions | 0.2 | 2.8 |
| Single parents' pensions | −1.4 | 5.6 |
| Unemployment insurance benefits | −2.5 | 5.0 |
| Invalid and childless widow benefits | 0.2 | 2.8 |

*Source*: Manning (1985: 125).

welfare expenditures under the Hawke government increased substantially compared with the expenditure under the Fraser government. As Table 4.1 shows, the increases were mainly in medical care and housing and, it is safe to say, benefited the population as a whole rather than producer interests *per se*. Table 4.2 points to a clear improvement in social benefits for non-producers under the Hawke government. True, the Accord has not led to a substantial drop in unemployment, a measure which would benefit persons other than those currently in the labour force despite the creation of a large number of new jobs. But at least the government has been spending more money on labour-market policies than its predecessor, which has helped to ease the problem of unemployment. As regards poverty, the government's selectivist approach has meant increased protection for those in need, at least in the short run. Perhaps the one exception to this are the unemployed, who have been a major target of welfare backlash and deterrence. Australia's unique form of selectivist unemployment benefits, financed from general taxes and with no limit on the duration of benefit, may have been an important reason for the backlash.

Overall, it seems misleading to pose the problem of equity and social justice under the Hawke government in terms of a conflict between producer and non-producer interests. Rather, the government and the Accord may be criticized for not doing enough to rebuild the welfare state and for giving in to the clamour for fiscal rectitude and for the reduction of public expenditure. The result is that *both* producers and non-producers pay in terms of inequity. Critics of social contract make much of the fact that, unlike organized workers and employers, non-producer groups, such as the aged, women not in the paid labour force, single parents and the disabled, are not 'represented' at the bargaining table. *Ipso facto* their interests are ignored. But to think of the social contract as a platform representing sectional interests is to devalue its significance for the non-propertied masses and also to distort its main purpose as an institution. Ironically, it is social scientists on the left – Marxists among them – who seem to balk at the suggestion that the organized trade union movement might be capable of something more than simply being the mouthpiece of its paid-up members. If we see the Accord as a part of the struggle against capital waged by the non-propertied class with the organized workforce as its core (albeit within the framework of welfare capitalism with all the limitations that this entails), then the idea of a producer and non-producer divide relating to the Accord virtually disappears.[85] What remains is a critique of a specific social contract and its policies. And here, let us concede, the Australian Accord has fallen far short of being a principled champion of the non-propertied classes or a master-builder of the welfare state. But how much of this can be laid at the door of the Accord as such and how much can be attributed to other factors, including Australian political and social welfare traditions, is a question that needs more careful attention than it has received so far.

## 92    The welfare state in capitalist society

## Notes and references

1. Despite official bilingualism, the French presence in Canada is primarily restricted to the single province of Quebec.
2. Courtney (1988: 198); Frizzell and Westell (1985: 95).
3. Sears (1985: 29–30); Frizzell and Westell (1985: 106–7).
4. Perlin (1988: 91–2); Frizzell and Westell (1985: 106).
5. Perlin (1988: 91–2).
6. Frizzell and Westell (1985: 103, 107); Courtney (1988: 198–9).
7. These ideas were spelled out in Canada (1984), a key policy document. On the government's volte-face after winning the election, see Bercuson et al. (1986: 94–5, 98–103).
8. On government strategy and initiatives, see Rice (1987: 216).
9. See Prince (1985: 8). For a more detailed analysis, see Prince (1986b).
10. Prince (1985: 8–9); Bercuson et al. (1986: ch. 6, passim).
11. On full-employment policy in North America see Apple (1980: 16–17, 29). Canada's unemployment rate for 1960–7 averaged 4.8% compared with the Britain's 1.5% and OECD Europe's 2.7% (see Table 6, Appendix 2). For 1960–82, it averaged 6.1% (US average 5.7%), the highest among industrialized OECD nations. For 1960–82, OECD-Europe averaged 4.3% and the European Economic Community 3.6%. See OECD (1984a: 39).
12. See, for example, Calvert (1984: 26–7, 70–1, 83–4); OECD (1976a: 25); OECD (1982b: 29–32, 43); OECD (1984b: 22).
13. Sears (1985: 35); Perlin (1988: 91).
14. Moscovitch (1986: 85); Lachapelle (1988: 246–8); 'Social spending to be slashed', The Globe and Mail (9 November 1984: 10).
15. Rice (1987: 224–5); Lachapelle (1988: 247).
16. Parliament (1987: 17).
17. Riches (1987: 133–40).
18. See 'Statement on Social Policy of Progressive Conservative Government', Perception, 1984, 8(I), p. 8; Perlin (1988: 92).
19. 'Deficit numbers belie Tory claims', The Globe and Mail (9 November 1984: 1) 'PM changes stand on social programs', The Globe and Mail (10 November 1984: 1–2).
20. Economic Council of Canada (1984: 27–33); Ternowetsky (1987: 377–83); Calvert (1984: ch. 6).
21. Canada (1984: 71).
22. Canada (1984: 71).
23. 'PM changes stand on social programs', The Globe and Mail (10 November 1984: 1).
24. 'PM changes stand on social programs', The Globe and Mail (10 November 1984: 1–2).
25. Bercuson et al. (1986: 106–10); Lachapelle (1988: 290–1).
26. Bercuson et al. (1986: 112–14).
27. Bercuson et al. (1986: 116).
28. Bercuson et al. (1986: 117–19).
29. Bercuson et al. (1986: 119); Prince (1986b: 43–8).

30. It should be remembered that since the early 1970s the Canadian tax system has increasingly favoured corporations and higher income groups. Thus when Conservatives came to power it was quite regressive. The Conservative government has added to the regressivity while implementing some equitable tax measures as well. On taxation in the 1970s and early 1980s see Calvert (1984: ch. 6); Ternowetsky (1987: 377–83). On more recent developments, see Prince (1986a: 32–4); Chorney and Molloy (1988: 206–27).
31. Kirwin (1986: 39).
32. 'The force that isn't', *The Globe and Mail* (8 June 1985: 6).
33. Wilson (1988: 35–8).
34. National Council of Welfare (1988: 7).
35. Moscovitch (1988: 292, 307).
36. Social Planning Council of Metropolitan Toronto (1986: 6); Armitage (1988: 178–9).
37. Riches (1987: 136–7); Armitage (1988: 180–2).
38. 'Canada's checkerboard social policy', *Perception* (May/August 1986: 3).
39. See pages 28–9 above for policies in the United States.
40. The rate of unemployment dropped from 11.3% in 1984 to 8.9% in 1986 and to below 8% in March 1989. The rate of poverty dropped from a peak of 17.3% in 1984 to 14.9% in 1986, close to the rate (14.7% in 1981) before the jump in unemployment in 1982. On unemployment see Table 1, Appendix 2. On poverty see National Council of Welfare (1988: 7). On taxes, transfers and the distribution of income, see National Council of Welfare (1988: 108–9); National Council of Welfare (1989: 4–7); Canadian Council on Social Development (1988: 1); Banting (1987).
41. It must be remembered, however, that fiscal restraint in social welfare in Canada is now more than a decade old. During their first term of office (1984–8), Conservatives maintained or intensified the restraint. Thus federal programme expenditure, including social expenditure but excluding debt charges fell from 19.5% of GDP in 1984–5 to a projected 16.1% in 1989–90. See 'Business failing to acknowledge deep cuts in federal government', *Toronto Star* (29 April 1989: D2). The recent budget (April 1989) makes extensive cuts in social programmes and expenditures. See 'The Federal Budget', *The Globe and Mail* (27 April 1989: A21–2).
42. See, for example, Magnusson *et al.* (1984: 11–12); Carroll (1984: 96); 'Socreds catch BC off guard', *The Globe and Mail* (20 July 1983: 9).
43. Wolfe (1985: 9); Bercuson *et al.* (1986: 37–9); Simeon (1988: 25–31). For a more critical view of Conservative governance, see Ternowetsky (1987: 373–6).
44. Prince (1986a: 4).
45. Prince (1986a: 4); Stanbury (1988: 119–20, 146–8).
46. On policy-making process in the two countries, see Kudrle and Marmor (1981: 81–121), Leman (1977) and Leman (1980: ch. 6).
47. On Australian social welfare see Graycar (1983); Kaim-Caudle (1973:

**94**    *The welfare state in capitalist society*

ch. ix, *passim* and pages 323–4). On Labour governments' plans and achievements, see Whitlam (1985: chs 1, 7 and 8); Wilenski (1980). See also Castles (1985).
48. Whitlam (1985: 346–7 and ch. 8, *passim*).
49. See, for example, Head (1982: 112–17), Elliot (1982: 124–32).
50. Stilwell (1986: 6–7, 10–11); Beilharz (1986: 211–14).
51. During 1983–6 some 700,000 new jobs were created. The annual rate of *increase* in employment between 1983–4 and 1986–7 was nearly four times that of the decade between 1973–4 and 1983–4. However, the labour force also grew at a faster rate in the mid-1980s, which in part explains why the rate of unemployment did not fall despite the high rate of job creation. See McDonald (1988: 47, Table 3).
52. Jamrozik (1987: 55).
53. The Hawke government has been spending considerably more on labour-market measures than its predecessor, the Frazer government. Measures such as the Community Employment Programme are helping the long-term unemployed and other disadvantaged workers (notably women and Aboriginals) find jobs. See Chapman (1985: 99–104).
54. Graycar (1983). See also references in note 47 above.
55. Jamrozik (1987: 59, 72); Beilharz (1986: 216).
56. Ilfe (1987: 84–9); Castles (1987: 95–8).
57. McCallum (1984); Carmichael and Plowman (1985: 139–40).
58. Carmichael and Plowman (1985: 134–6; 142–3); Stilwell (1986: 17–18).
59. Nurick (1987: 120).
60. Saunders (1987b: 13).
61. Saunders (1987b: 14).
62. OECD (1988c: 12).
63. OECD (1987b: 10).
64. OECD (1988c: 13).
65. On social security, see Saunders (1987a: 411). On social expenditure more generally, see OECD (1985b: 21), which shows that Australia spent a lower proportion of its GNP on social welfare than Britain, the United States, Canada and New Zealand. Among industrialized OECD countries, only Japan and Switzerland spent less (OECD: 1985b: 21).
66. Saunders (1987a: 416).
67. On the Tax Summit see Stilwell (1986: 15–16); on changes in taxation, see OECD (1987b: 9–10).
68. Saunders (1987a: 419). In 1985 nearly one-half of Australia's tax revenue came from income taxes. Only two industrialized OECD countries, Denmark and New Zealand, relied more heavily on income taxes than Australia. See McKee (1987–8: 33).
69. Saunders (1987a: 418–21). The 'trilogy' of fiscal commitment by the government included the promise not to increase taxation as a proportion of GDP. See, for example, Stilwell (1986: 14–18).
70. Jamrozik (1987: 71); Castles (1987: 96–7); Stilwell (1986: 77–8).

71. Howe (1987: 8).
72. See, however, Bradbury *et al.* (1986); Saunders (1987b: 19–20).
73. Saunders (1987b: 22). According to one estimate, the proportion of households in poverty rose from 11.5% to 12.4% between 1981–2 and 1985–6. See Browne (1987: 34–5). Johnson (1988: 21) estimates a rise in poverty from 10.5% to 13.0% of all income units.
74. Cass (1987: 171–2).
75. Cass (1987: 171–2). See also Vipond *et al.* (1987), which suggests a strong association between unemployment and poverty in the early 1980s.
76. Cass (1987: 175).
77. Saunders (1987b: 25–6). In 1987 the Hawke government's election platform included a pledge to abolish child poverty by 1990 through a 'family package' of additional resources. See Saunders and Whiteford (1987).
78. Saunders (1987b: 42).
79. OECD (1988c: 18; McDonald (1988: 43).
80. See Chapter 1, note 4.
81. See Esping-Andersen (1985) for a general overview. See Castles (1985) for a distinctive view of the peculiarities of Australian developments.
82. Schott (1987: 53).
83. McIntyre (1986: 13).
84. See McDonald (1988: 43, 49) for the decline in wages. The share of wages and salaries in the national income fell from 64.0% in 1982–3 to 59.3% in 1985–6. Despite cutbacks in social expenditures after 1985, the share of social expenditures in GDP was undoubtedly higher in 1986–7 than in 1982–3 when the Labour government assumed office. See, for example, Stilwell (1986: 52, 70–1). It cannot be accounted for by increased social problems, e.g. higher unemployment.
85. This is broadly in line with Walter Korpi's notion of tripartism and social contract as expressions of democratic class-struggle and societal bargaining (see pages 114–16 below). On Australia, see Stilwell (1986: ch. 3).

# 5

# The welfare state after the 'crisis'

The history of the post-war welfare state can usefully be divided into three more or less distinct periods. The first spans roughly the period 1950–75. During this period the welfare state as defined and understood in this book – in short, the Keynesian welfare state (KWS) – became established as a stable and dominant paradigm of social development in the West. The second, which spans roughly the period 1975–80, was a period of 'crisis' when welfare capitalism went into disequilibrium. Conditions naturally varied from one country to another and this made for a range of experience – from mild to severe – of discontinuity and dislocation. The resulting strain, tension and economic anomie led to a crisis of confidence in the viability of the KWS. The third period began around 1980 with the election of the Thatcher and Reagan governments on a platform which broke ideologically with the KWS in favour of a neo-conservative approach. This marks the beginning of the 'post-crisis' period during which the KWS was relativized as a paradigm of advanced capitalist society. Neo-conservatism on the right and social corporatism on the left have emerged, then, as alternative approaches to, or at least as distinct departures from, the KWS.

We have examined neo-conservative and social-corporatist models in action in two pairs of 'hard-core' regimes, namely those in the United Kingdom and in the United States, on the one hand, and in Sweden and Austria, on the other. We have sought to demonstrate that significant policy differences exist between these two groups of countries which have considerable implications for inequality and for social welfare more generally. No doubt, among other things, the constraints of an electoral democracy have served to limit the extent of change in neo-conservative regimes. These regimes have had to abandon hopes of a direct assault on social expenditures and programmes in light of adverse electoral consequences. In this respect the idea of entitlement, i.e. the social rights of citizenship and its institutionalization through universal social programmes – major developments of the period since the Second World War – have largely withstood the onslaught of neo-conservative ideology and policy orientation. None the less, as we have argued, the potential of neo-conservative regimes for eroding mainstream services cannot be underestimated. In particular, these regimes have abandoned the commitment to full employment, to the prevention of poverty and to the maintenance of a national minimum standard of living more broadly defined. Seen in conjunction with changes in taxation policy, the weakening of trade union rights and human rights more generally, these regimes stand for principles and practices which depart significantly from those of the KWS. The post-war welfare state represented a commitment to a one-nation democracy based on universal rights of citizenship; neo-conservative policy represents a return to the two-nation society of the past. Indeed, the development towards a dual society and a dual economy reminiscent of the situation in the Third World seems well under way in the United States and the United Kingdom. It is important to note, however, that this dualization of society has not cost these regimes electorally. They have achieved economic growth, price stability and some degree of economic modernization. They have also garnered enough electoral support to continue as neo-conservative regimes. In short, they remain politically viable and economically progressive regimes.

Social-corporatist regimes in Sweden and Austria, on the other hand, have sought to maintain the commitment to the three basic elements of the welfare state – full employment, universal social services, and the maintenance of a basic minimum standard of living. True, these regimes have had to come to terms with the fact that the welfare state operates within the framework of a privately-owned and profit-oriented market economy. None the less, in differing ways the social policies of Sweden and Austria since the mid-1970s and their implications for equity and social justice show what can be done towards maintaining the basic commitment to the welfare state. There is no evidence to suggest that economic growth and efficiency have suffered as a result of the policy of maintaining high levels of employment and social expenditures. In particular, Sweden's labour market policy emerges as an effective means of achieving flexibility and adaptation to technological change without sacrificing social justice. Despite gloomy prognostications from both the right and the left, the basic tripartite institutions of cooperation such as the Social Partnership in Austria and the Labour Market Board in Sweden remain largely intact. True, in place of the broad consensus and truce over social and economic policies there is a greater degree of conflict, and at least in Austria, there seems to be a general drift to the right. In Sweden the consensual mechanisms of collective bargaining and industrial relations are under strain. All the same, it cannot be denied that social corporatism, though chastened, has survived a long period of economic uncertainty and poor growth. What is more, there is little evidence of a tax–welfare backlash or of a revolt against the welfare state and its bureaucracy in either Sweden or Austria. Admittedly, the expansion of social welfare programmes and expenditures is not on the cards but neither is the retrenchment of what exists. Considering that earlier pre-crisis policies concerning taxation, industrial relations and human rights have remained in place, the economic crisis of the 1970s and its aftermath has not resulted in more than a marginal increase in inequality. The social costs of capitalist economic development have not been allowed to fall on those least able to shoulder them.

We also examined Canada and Australia as prospective sites for the 'diffusion' of these two policy orientations. In different ways these two countries highlight the importance of national variations both in the extent to which policy models may be emulated and in their outcome. In Canada the flirtation of Conservatives with the neo-conservative social policy of retrenchment, followed by a hasty retreat, points to the continuing popularity and support for universal mainstream programmes. It also suggests that politics matters, as electoral considerations remain paramount in Canada for Conservatives who were in opposition for the best part of the twenty years preceding their victory in 1984. They have not been willing to risk electoral unpopularity by embarking on a neo-conservative social agenda even though pressure from business to move in that direction has been and remains quite strong. The Mulroney government's brief attempt to tamper with universal programmes followed by a retreat seems to confirm what we found in Britain and the United States – that the nation-wide constituency for universal programmes makes them difficult to retrench. Further evidence of the unwillingness of the Canadian government to move in a neo-conservative direction is shown by the fact that programmes which serve unpopular minorities, for example general welfare assistance, have not been singled out for cutbacks as they have in the United States – at least not directly. It has to be remembered, however, that under Liberal governments Canada managed quite successfully to reduce social expenditure, lower wages, increase unemployment and curb inflation. In this context, short of engineering an ideological shift of national consensus to the right, it was not easy to make a strong case for neo-conservatism of the Reagan and Thatcher variety.

In 1988 the Conservatives won a second term of office in Canada. Neither their election campaign nor their party platform suggests a renewed effort to move social policy along the neo-conservative path. The major electoral issue projected by the Conservatives was the free trade treaty with the United States; the new government has now legislated free trade. Its implications for jobs and social programmes, though hotly debated, remain somewhat uncertain. Apart from the prospect of job losses, it is feared that closer economic integration with the United States will exert a downward pressure on social protection and other measures to bring them more in line with those that exist in the United States. It is, of course, conceivable that change could also be in the other direction. But given the economic disparity between the two countries and the decimation of labour unions in the United States such an outcome is highly improbable.

In Canada the free trade initiative has been seen as a Trojan horse which will enable neo-conservative social policy to be implemented indirectly as a part of a larger economic agenda. Such a reading of the situation is in line with the perspective of this book – based on class and ideology – which warns us not to underestimate neo-conservatism. Indeed, quite apart from free trade, the government is once again planning to reduce the deficit through substantial reductions in social expenditure. That, too, would be in keeping with the class-interest perspective of this book. Be that as it may, developments in Canada during 1984–8 have been along conservative rather than neo-conservative lines as far as social welfare is concerned. As in the United Kingdom and the United States, albeit in a different economic and political context, democracy has acted as a brake on the encroachments of capital.

In Australia the Accord reached in 1983 between a Labour government and the trade unions must be seen as a significant event. That the Accord remains in place spanning the life of three parliaments makes it more so. First, it shows that a social contract can help sustain social democracy and social welfare. This becomes clear when we contrast developments in Australia with the fortunes of the Labour Party and the welfare state in Britain since the late 1970s. A contrast with the reversals of social democratic policy and politics in France since the advent of the Mitterrand government in 1981 tells pretty much the same story. Moreover, Australia's own experience under an earlier Labour government led by Gough Whitlam shows the difficulty of retaining office and seeking to build a welfare state in the absence of a social contract with organized labour.

Second, Australia shows that the social-corporatist approach can work, however modest its scope and achievements in countries outside its *locus classicus* in continental Europe. After the débâcle of the Callaghan government and the social contract in Britain, the Australian labour movement's success in sustaining a government with some commitment to improving social welfare and to building a welfare state in the long run cannot be dismissed lightly.

Third, it is also clear that general models such as social corporatism operate within nation-states each of which has a unique history and trajectory of development. The import of things Scandinavian cannot turn Australia into another Sweden. This is where national differences come in. Here historical legacies such as the relative strength of labour and capital, the nature of political parties and the pattern of social welfare institutions acquire critical importance. As we have seen, in the context of more than thirty years of Conservative rule and a uniquely selectivist pattern of social welfare, five years of social democracy and Accord have yielded only modest achievements in repairing and rebuilding the welfare state. Undoubtedly the Hawke government has been extremely cautious – indeed conservative – in many of its policies. In its attempt to balance the claims of welfare and capitalism, it has sided increasingly with the latter. Economic development and the modernization of Australia within the context of a market economy seem to have been granted the major priority. There is an interesting parallel between the Hawke government and the Mulroney Conservatives in Canada. Like Canadian Conservatives only more so, the Australian Labour Party has also spent many years in opposition. Winning elections and retaining office have weighed heavily with the government. Moreover, Labour came to power in a situation which would be comparable, say, to the British Labour Party winning office at the end of the Thatcher era. It, too, would have to contend with the legacy of large-scale unemployment and a lean and mean social welfare system. The task of transforming such a situation into that of a full-employment welfare state would be a daunting and protracted one.

Fourth, and finally, the Australian case shows quite clearly that the social contract and other forms of voluntary agreement between major economic interests do little more than provide an institutional framework for decision-making. The actual decisions made, the trade-offs arrived at and the bargains struck are not determined by the institutions of social contract *per se*. Rather, they depend on the nature of civil society. This includes a host of factors pertaining to the social structure. Australia is not Sweden and it is not to be expected that the Accord might transform Australian welfare capitalism into a Swedish-style welfare state. But compared with its Conservative predecessor (the Fraser government was in office from 1975 to 1983) the Hawke government at the very least must be seen as the lesser of two evils.

More generally, Australian social corporatism compares favourably not only with the neo-conservative alternative *à la* Reagan or Thatcher, but perhaps also with the more traditional approach of the French Parti Socialiste. As we know, that led to a strong radical stance at first only to be followed by a volte-face, bringing in its wake disillusionment with social democracy and in particular with its ability to enhance the welfare element in welfare capitalism (see page 14 above).

However, this is not to underestimate the potential hazards of corporatism. In many ways the Australian situation is moving closer to a position where the Accord secures labour acquiescence to increasingly pro-capital policies accompanied by substantial cutbacks in social welfare. Not surprisingly, from both ends of the political spectrum the Hawke government has been compared to the Thatcher government, and not without some justification.[1] It is clear, as Korpi and others have argued, that the outcome of social corporatism does not depend on social corporatism *per se* (see page 61 above).

## Current interpretations of the welfare state

From the vantage point of the 1980s Max Weber's view of the social sciences – that God has granted them eternal youth – seems most apposite. Those of us who had the good fortune (or misfortune) to live through the tumultuous days of the 1950s and 1960s, studded with stars in the firmament of social theory – such as Talcott Parsons and Louis Althusser – will recognize the sad wisdom of Weber's observation. Grand theories of the 1950s and 1960s – with their pretensions of 'scientific' sociology and 'scientific' Marxism – seem to have vanished like a bad dream leaving 'not a rack behind'. Or rather their memory lingers, largely as an embarrassment, a reminder of the follies of yesteryear. Pragmatism, modest hypotheses based on correlations, empiricism, common sense or plain silence seem to be the order of the day, at least as far as the welfare state is concerned. Perhaps Kierkegaard's aphorism that we are condemned to 'live forwards but understand backwards' sums up the situation of the social sciences neatly. At any rate, the events of the 1970s (primarily economic) and their aftermath (primary political) were so much at odds with the conventional wisdom of post-war social science – Marxist and non-Marxist – that the advent of neo-conservative regimes and their ideological break with the post-war consensus over welfare capitalism caused a state of considerable confusion if not panic, especially on the left. Whether the welfare state would survive the neo-conservative assault became an urgent question.

Out of the speculations and the unfolding of events of the last decade have emerged three viewpoints on the welfare state which we shall examine: those of irreversibility, maturity, and welfare pluralism. What follows is essentially a critical examination of these interpretations in light of the arguments and evidence presented in this study. We shall also refer briefly to what may be called the democratic class-struggle thesis associated with Scandinavian socialists such as Korpi and Esping-Andersen which seems a much better guide to contemporary developments. With some simplification we could claim these to be the main interpretations of the welfare state in the 1980s and beyond.

### Irreversibility thesis

We have discussed this thesis at some length in Chapter 2 (see pages 32–42). Here we shall do no more than summarize briefly why we find it inadequate as a guide to understanding the changes that the welfare state has undergone in recent years. Substantive as well as methodological issues are involved:

1.  The reversible/irreversible dichotomy is cast in such global and exclusive terms that it cannot do justice to the partial changes and partial reversals suffered by the welfare state under neo-conservative regimes.
2.  The welfare state tends to be equated with levels of social or even public expenditure. As we have argued (pages 33–4) the public finance view of social change leaves out of account a great deal that is important. The idea that the social welfare system is being 'restructured' rather than dismantled by these regimes fares somewhat better but it, too, is inadequate in that it fails to capture the specifics of the change, especially from the viewpoint of individual life chances and inequities.
3.  Full employment tends to be left out of the definition of the post-war welfare state. The end of full employment and, in particular, the neo-conservative policy of using unemployment as a device for curbing inflation and driving down wages are not taken into account when considering whether or not the welfare state has suffered a reversal. By the same token, the struggle to maintain full employment does not feature as a part of the alternative policy followed by social-corporatist regimes.
4.  Changes in taxation policy and in the pattern of financing social expenditure are rarely seen as a reversal of pre-crisis policy. The impact of fiscal policies on poverty and on the future of state welfare therefore tends to be left out of account.
5.  The irreversibility thesis focuses on material and institutional aspects, i.e. on changes in social programmes and expenditures, and virtually ignores change at the level of ideology.

True, popular attitudes and public opinion concerning the welfare state have received a great deal of attention and show continuing support for social programmes. On the other hand, social and political ideologies relevant to the welfare state, notably neo-conservatism, and their influence on policy-makers and others have received little attention. There has been a tendency on the part of neo-Marxists and others to dismiss the ideology of the new right as largely rhetoric and wishful thinking. In our view this is a serious error (see pages 36–7 above). While it is important to distinguish between professed ideology, on the one hand, and institutional or material change, on the other, change must be investigated at both levels. The influence of ideology on the practice of neo-conservatism, however indirect and gradual, remains important. The Thatcher government, for example, has shown quite clearly that its ideology is not mere idle chatter. Over the long haul it has moved systematically, if cautiously, in the direction indicated by that ideology. Indeed, if the situation is seen in terms of the class interests of capital and the propertied groups, then the role of ideology and its importance becomes obvious.

6.  Irreversibility theorists rarely take the temporal dimension into account when considering social change. There may be good grounds for suggesting that the welfare state is irreversible in the *short run*. But the claim that it is also irreversible in the *long run* requires reasoning of a different kind. The significance of this distinction has received scant recognition. In any case, there has been a tendency to underestimate the potential for the erosion of social welfare in countries such as the United Kingdom and the United States.

7.  Since the problem of reversibility tends to be posed in terms of simple dichotomy – 'capitalism versus democracy', 'capital versus labour' or 'government versus the electorate' – the problem of stratification and its relationship to change has not received the attention it deserves. As Korpi and others have shown (see page 41 above) social programmes serve different groups of people and therefore differ in the degree of support they receive. A 'divide and rule' retrenchment strategy is based on exploiting such differences as well as differences in the market capacity of different classes. In short, a proper under-standing of these issues requires a dynamic perspective on

change – one which is sensitive to distributional conflict and class struggle. Such a perspective has largely been missing from the irreversibility thesis.[2]

8. Lastly, the belief that the welfare state is a functional necessity of capitalism, although not heard recently, has been implicit at least in the neo-Marxist argument of irreversibility.[3] Since functionalism, whether of the right or the left, and its problems have been debated at length in post-war social science, no general comment on functionalism *per se* will be made here. A specific comment must suffice.

The argument that capitalism cannot do without the paraphernalia of social programmes, though it cannot live in peace with them either, needs *at the very least* to demonstrate that there are no adequate functional *substitutes* to publicly provided education, health care, income security and so on. Since this has not been done (at least to my knowledge), arguments implicit or otherwise of 'functional necessity' must be treated as unfounded assertions. However, implicit here is an important point related to the time-scale of change (see point 6 above). The point is that moving from publicly provided services to a functional substitute, for example from state to occupational pensions, *involves a time-lag*. Hence the functions of social welfare make social programmes a virtual necessity in the short run. Therefore, they cannot be abolished overnight. However – and this is the important point – they *can* be abolished over a longer period of time as functional substitutes are found and put in place. This is the significance of privatization and the underfunding of social programmes.

To conclude: the irreversibility thesis fails to take into account and do justice to a host of important changes that the welfare state has undergone since the mid-1970s. In the following form, however, the thesis is both useful and acceptable: given the various functions of accumulation and legitimation that state welfare services perform, given the vested interests involved and given also electoral competition and democratic institutions, these services are unlikely to be abolished *en masse* in capitalist societies and certainly not within a short span of time. Put in this form, the thesis takes into account the possibility of relatively minor changes occurring in the short run and more substantial changes in the long run.

## The welfare state as a mature institution

Some social scientists see the welfare state of the 1980s as a stable and mature institution of Western industrial societies. What has happened in recent years, they argue, is that the welfare state has stopped growing. On the other hand, it is not really being retrenched. Rather, the situation is one of stability. In this perspective the fear of a substantial retrenchment voiced in the 1970s appears as the obverse side of the unrealistic expectation current in the 1960s, namely, that of an ever expanding welfare state. Heclo, a major exponent of this view, suggests that the Western welfare state has developed through four stages: experimentation (1870s–1920s), consolidation (1930s–1940s), expansion (1950s–60s), and, most recently, reformulation (1970s and beyond).[4]

Heclo points out that neo-conservatives have not succeeded in rolling back the welfare state. On the other hand the automatic expansion of the welfare state in the 1960s, which was largely a product of the extraordinary and unprecedented economic growth in Western democracies, has also come to an end. The 'growth state' made hard choices between economic and social values unnecessary. But as the runaway growth scenario disappeared in the 1970s, a reformulation of the welfare state became necessary. Although Heclo is somewhat unclear on the nature of this reformulation, he foresees a new 'mix' in the values of liberty, equality and security.[5] Essentially it is a situation in which the basic institutions of the welfare state remain in place but further growth becomes questionable. Writing before Thatcher and Reagan took office, Heclo observes:

> Nowhere is there evidence of major welfare state programs being dismantled. What can be seen here and there among the Western democracies are efforts to slow down some expenditures' growth rates, to institute more cost controls, to refrain from undertaking major new social policy commitments, or to stretch out their implementation over time.[6]

The Reagan 'revolution' seems not to have impressed Heclo overmuch. Despite ideology and rhetoric, much of what was there before Reagan remains standing. Indeed,

> Reaganism will eventually be seen to have helped conserve a

predominantly status quo, middle-class welfare state. It will have done
so by making the existing system work in a more disciplined, or at least a
more broadly acceptable way to the American public.[7]

On the other side of the Atlantic, Klein and O'Higgins also find that
despite 'the political rhetoric of rollback and the extent of economic
disruption, the attack on social policies has, in most countries, been
largely blunted'.[8] The major social programmes are now 'a part of
the day-to-day reality and expectation of the population', a part of
the status quo with all the resistance to change that that implies.[9]
Klein and O'Higgins endorse Heclo's view that social policies are
not in a period of 'crisis' but of reformulation.[10] What we now have
are enduring, mature institutions of social welfare and what we
need is 'a new set of ideas to allow us to consider problems of
adaptation and change in mature institutions'.[11] As John Myles has
pointed out, it is somewhat ironic that proclamations of maturity
have come from countries such as the United States and the United
Kingdom, countries which could scarcely claim to have the most
developed or 'mature' social welfare systems. (Does Australia, too,
belong to mature welfare states?) Clearly, what these social
scientists mean is that in their own countries and more generally,
the present level of social expenditures and services seems to
represent the ceiling of what might be expected in the foreseeable
future. The implication is that instead of crying 'wolf' – whether
about 'crisis' or 'retrenchment' – we should focus on important tasks
at hand such as the effective management of a given level of
resources to achieve greater flexibility and adaptation.

There are a number of problems with the idea of a more or less
steady state in social welfare. First, social welfare institutions do not
exist in a vacuum removed from the economic and social realities of
the society of which they are a part. The static scenario of maturity
and stability seems to look on change as either marginal or
insignificant. Thus Klein and O'Higgins are not unaware of the role
of ideology in giving incremental change a qualitative dimension.
But their emphasis remains very much on 'management', 'adaptation' and 'flexibility', as if these were politically neutral measures
though which policy managers could operate a 'rational', if
somewhat circumscribed, social welfare system. The assumption
here seems to be that of a broad social consensus over social policy.
Yet it is plain that neo-conservative policies in the United Kingdom
and the United States, far from being technocratic, have been quite

openly class-oriented and ideological. Lacking a class and distributional perspective – important for making sense of the 'post-crisis' situation – the maturity thesis misses out on the significance of the New Right and what it has already accomplished. More generally, the points we made against the irreversibility thesis (see pages 103–5 above) by and large apply also to the mature-welfare-state argument. For example, neither the end of full employment nor changes in taxation and fiscal policies feature in what these writers see as the welfare state. While Heclo as well as Klein and O'Higgins acknowledge the importance of ideology, they do not seem to appreciate, or at least not sufficiently, its implications for the erosion of social welfare over the long haul. No doubt the task of keeping public services flexible and adaptive in the absence of growth is an important problem. It is also true that assertions of a continuing 'crisis' of the welfare state now need to be laid to rest. But that does not mean that we should ignore or play down the changes in social policy – understood somewhat broadly – that are being wrought by neo-conservative regimes.

### Welfare pluralism: from welfare state to welfare society

The 'welfare society' perspective is associated with writers such as Martin Rein and Lee Rainwater in the United States and Richard Rose in Britain.[12] Many other names can, of course, be claimed for this school of thought, especially if it is seen as broadly synonymous with the idea of 'welfare pluralism' or the mixed economy of welfare.[13]

Stated simply, the basic proposition underlying this approach is that 'welfare' – goods and services which satisfy basic needs and afford social protection – derives from a multitude of sources: the state, the market (including the enterprise), voluntary and charitable organizations and the kinship network (including the household). To equate social welfare with state welfare is therefore to ignore all of these other sources of social protection and support. Total welfare in a society is a sum of these parts. The diminution of one of the welfare sectors does not necessarily mean a net loss of welfare.[14] It may be simply a matter of moving the provision of welfare from one sector to another. Thus what has been happening in Western countries recently is primarily a shift away from the pre-eminence of the state in the overall scheme of welfare. A redistribution of functions among the various suppliers of welfare is taking place, while the general level of welfare would remain pretty much the same. The state may withdraw from direct provision, encouraging employers, voluntary agencies, households and others to increase their effort.

Interestingly then, what we have here is almost another version of the thesis of irreversibility – this time not of the welfare state, which is seen as shrinking somewhat, but that of social welfare itself. It is as though at a given stage in society's development welfare resources constitute a fixed quantity and it is largely a matter of dividing up the welfare function among the various suppliers. What is happening at this moment, then, should be seen not as the retrenchment of welfare but as a reallocation of tasks among the different suppliers. Rose, for instance, warns us against

> the fallacious assumption that a reduction in state provision of welfare is necessarily a reduction in welfare in society. If Scandinavia is a model of what the state can do to provide welfare (and what citizens will pay taxes for), then Japan is a counter example of how a society can do without high levels of public provision, yet have a population that is educated, healthy and secure in old age.[15]

Rein and Rainwater are also impressed by what they see as the 'blurring of sectoral boundaries' between the public and private spheres in welfare. What is needed, therefore, is a holistic approach which examines all forms of social protection independent of the sector in which they are administered, financed and controlled.[16] The politics of welfare, according to these writers, is now very much a politics of shifting costs from one sector to another. After reviewing studies of sick pay and pension arrangements from a number of countries, Rein and Rainwater conclude that 'private occupational welfare does not automatically lead to perverse redistribution and the growth of inequalities. Much depends on how and why privatization is introduced.'[17]

It is instructive to note the normative distance between Titmuss's pioneering analysis of the 'social division of welfare'[18] which referred to state, fiscal and occupational welfare, undertaken over thirty years ago as a critique of pluralism, and the decidedly benign evaluations of the 'welfare mix' by welfare pluralists today. Implicitly or explicitly, then, recent changes in the welfare state, notably in neo-conservative countries, are seen more or less as changes in the *form* in which welfare is supplied. Often the reduced role of the state in welfare is viewed with approval as it may result in a more decentralized and plural form of welfare mix. To quote Rose again, a 'crisis of the welfare state is not a crisis of welfare in society. In mixed societies, families have a multiplicity of ways to maintain their welfare.'[19] Indeed, 'total welfare in society is likely to be greater if there are multiple sources rather than a single monopoly supplier'.[20] In a similar vein, Ken Judge rejects the view that in Thatcher's Britain 'the state is abdicating responsibility for promoting individual and collective welfare'.[21] However sincere their underlying concern, such views 'reflect a pervasive lack of intellectual and political imagination' in that welfare is equated with state welfare. In fact social policy in the United Kingdom is moving 'from a predominantly collectivist ethos towards a more viable conception of the state as an enabler'.[22] The 'enabling' state puts more emphasis on 'financing, planning, promoting and regulating services than it does on producing and delivering them'.[23]

What are we to make of this view of the changing welfare state? First, let us note that the pluralist argument does not apply to the decline of the full-employment welfare state and to the growth of substantial unemployment in Western countries. It is not easy to see what non-governmental substitutes there might be for the role of the government, which has been largely that of the 'enabling' kind in maintaining employment through a variety of policies, including labour-market measures. We may note in passing that while Judge, a British welfare pluralist, evokes the Beveridgian notion of a partnership between statutory and voluntary sectors in support of pluralism, he fails to mention full employment and to consider its implications for the idea of a national minimum – as part of the Beveridgian conception of social welfare.[24] Second, while welfare pluralists are right in pointing out that any overall assessment of social protection in a particular society must take non-state forms of welfare into account, they tend to gloss over the implications of shifting from one form of social welfare to another.

The point is that forms of welfare cannot simply be regarded as 'functional equivalents'. They are based on different principles and they differ in scope. The welfare mix is more than just a question of deciding who can do what best in terms of comparative advantage in the production of welfare services.[25] In this context it is important to distinguish between the *ends* and *means* of social welfare, that is, the principle of social welfare as *entitlement* to an adequate income or standard of service which can only be guaranteed by the government, and the most effective means of the *delivery* or supply of such services. In any case, both the ends and the means of social welfare involve conflict of various kinds – concerning values as well as interests. Pluralists tend to ignore these issues. For example, shifting the burden of care of the disabled and the frail elderly from the public sector to the household (read: women) is likely to have major implications for gender inequality.[26] It is, perhaps, the failure to distinguish between *disentitlement* to services, on the one hand, and the *privatization* of the *supply* of services, on the other, that enables pluralists to argue that the changes taking place in Britain or the United States are chiefly a matter of rearranging the division of labour in social welfare. In practice, disentitlement and privatization cannot be distinguished clearly. They overlap and interact. But the analytical distinction between the two is important and must be maintained. Much of the change outlined and discussed in this book is concerned with issues of entitlement seen implicitly as distinct from the question of auspices or the mode of service delivery. It is one thing to decentralize and privatize service delivery in such a way that entitlement is not weakened. It is quite another to 'privatize', that is, withdraw public services and public commitment to maintaining standards, without underwriting entitlement or ensuring that equity considerations are met.

In any case, none of the pluralists seems to have examined the changes brought about by the Thatcher and Reagan regimes in any detail to show that other sectors have picked up the tab when government has withdrawn from social welfare. Indeed, available evidence points the other way.[27] For example, as far as major cutbacks in the United States are concerned – general welfare, Medicaid and food stamps – the main functional substitute is private charity (unless it is assumed, in the manner of neo-conservative ideology, that government withdrawal of public assistance will make individuals or families work harder or help each other more, or that neighbours will become more neighbourly). Since charity is voluntary action, the giver has no obligation to give. The nature and scope of assistance remains unspecified and uncertain. Conversely, those in need do not have any *right* or *entitlement* to assistance from private sources and must be grateful for what they may receive. It seems almost verging on the obscene to suggest that what has been happening the United States and the United Kingdom is a mere rearranging of furniture in the drawing-room. As this book has tried to demonstrate, cutbacks in social programmes, the increase in unemployment and low-wage employment, and changes in taxation have together increased poverty and inequality considerably in neo-conservative regimes. This amounts to a net reduction in welfare if the latter is understood in terms of equity and a national minimum standard. What the 'mixed economy of welfare' approach shows clearly, if unwittingly, is the fact that the notion of 'welfare' is value-laden. The cause of the welfare state debate would be better served if welfare pluralists were to make their value standpoint clearer.[28]

Forms of social provision, then, differ in important ways, so that they cannot be considered as mere substitutes for one another. There is one other point. The government or the state sector is not merely a supplier of welfare. It is also the legitimate regulatory agency of societal values and activities. The state's role as *supplier* of welfare needs to be distinguished from its role as the *regulator* of welfare. Retrenchment and disentitlement are about the latter. The shrinkage of the state's role in the former sense is quite distinct from its withdrawal in the latter sense. Unfortunately, pluralist literature tends to conflate the state's dual role as regulator and as supplier so that disentitlement cannot be distinguished from the privatization of supply. The problem is further confounded by the fact that many on the left who wish to strengthen the government's role *vis-à-vis* entitlement are at the same time in favour of decentralized and non-statist forms of service delivery.[29] The distinction between collective *responsibility* for meeting needs and the *forms of delivery* employed as means is crucial in understanding recent developments. However, it is so often confounded that it merits some further attention. Figure 1 presents this relationship in a diagrammatic form.

The Keynesian model of the post-war welfare state tended to be highly state-centred in its conception of administration and service delivery. Indeed, there was a tendency to equate collective responsibility for minimum standards of equity and social protection, in short universality of entitlement, with state supply of services. In point of fact there is no reason why optimal state responsibility for maintaining minimum standards cannot go hand in hand with a great deal of devolution and pluralism in service delivery. What a two-dimensional approach requires is that any argument for welfare pluralism must situate itself on both dimensions. Failing that, there remains a great deal of confusion about what is meant by the 'mixed economy of welfare' or welfare pluralism with respect to entitlement and equity.

It is possible to illustrate this point by contrasting the United States with the Netherlands. In 1981 the Netherlands devoted 36.1% of its GDP to social welfare, compared with 20.8% in the United States, and was among the top spenders on social welfare.[30] At the same time the Netherlands had one of the most decentralized and plural systems of service delivery in the Western world, based historically on religious divisions within the nation.[31] Decentralization, pluralism and non-state forms of service delivery and administration nevertheless coexist with a high level of public expenditure and collective responsibility for maintaining a national minimum standard. The United States, too, has a mixed economy of welfare and a high degree of welfare pluralism, but of a different kind. The government spends far less on social welfare and assumes far less responsibility for maintaining national minimum standards in respect of income, health, housing, education and personal social welfare.[32] In Figure 1, the Netherlands represents the institutional/pluralist mix while the United States is more akin to the

|  | Y |  |
|---|---|---|
|  | Centralized/state-centred |  |
| Social democracy/ corporatism |  | Traditional conservatism |
| High ('institutional') |  | Low ('residual') |
|  |  | X |
| Libertarian socialism/ communism |  | Neo-conservatism |
|  | Decentralized/pluralist |  |

The X-axis represents collective responsibility for social security and equity, the Y-axis organization and delivery of services.

**Figure 1**   Social welfare: a two-dimensional view

residual/pluralist mix. There are, of course, many other distinctions that need to be made within the 'mix' of welfare pluralism. However, the main point to be emphasized is that the question of centralism versus pluralism in the organization and delivery of social services needs to be distinguished from greater or lesser collective responsibility for underwriting a national minimum. Neo-conservative countries have seen a shift on the policy dimension from institutional towards residual together with a shift away from centralized or statist towards decentralized and privatized service delivery systems. It is the former type of change that the thesis of 'welfare pluralism' or the 'welfare society' argument tends to gloss over.

## The democratic class struggle

The view that the welfare state is a product of democratic class struggle (DCS) is associated, above all, with social scientists such as Korpi, Stephens and Esping-Andersen.[33] It differs from pluralist interpretations of democratic polity in that it sees class conflict, especially that between capital and labour, as a major determinant of social policy in capitalist democracies. On the other hand, it also differs from those Marxist views of power which see the working-class struggle within capitalism as no more than defensive and working-class power as severely limited by the rule of capital. For Marxists corporatism is largely a means of securing the compliance of wage-earners to an incomes policy and a means of coopting organized labour within a framework of capitalist interests. The DCS perspective sees tripartism as a form of – and a moment in – the ongoing struggle between owners of capital and the working classes; as an aspect of 'societal bargaining' in which the outcome is not predetermined. In particular, it places a great deal of emphasis on the mobilization of power resources by labour primarily through organizing an increasingly higher proportion of wage-earners in unions and using its strength collectively, as a class, in order to engage in societal bargaining. The variation in welfare state policies of capitalist democracies can thus be understood largely in terms of the politics of class-conflict.[34]

Perhaps the most important idea – often explicit in the DCS perspective – is the potential of the labour movement for articulating an alternative vision and a workable collectivist model of society and being able to realize it, even if only in part, through concerted action. It is a vision which partakes of universalism and solidarity and seeks to go beyond the individualism and interest-group pluralism endemic in capitalist democracies. No other social movement seems to have the scope, continuity and resources of the organized labour movement.

As will have been evident throughout, this book has been influenced a good deal by the DCS perspective. Apart from emphasizing the politics of choice, conflict and change in social welfare – centred on class interests and the mobilization of labour – the DCS also takes account of the interplay between institutions and groups. Thus full employment and universal social services are seen not only as a product of working-class struggle. They are also seen as having a feedback in that they, in turn, help sustain the relative power position of the non-propertied classes in their struggle against the insecurities of the marketplace and the rule of capital.[35]

Moreover, the DCS perspective is sensitive to differences in social welfare policies (for example, universal or selective) and, while emphasizing the role of the organized working class, it takes full account of the differing interests of social strata in relation to the welfare state.[36] While in many ways this book has offered an interpretation that is theoretically open-ended, its debt to the DCS perspective is, or should be, fairly evident. At the very least, the DCS perspective has performed a valuable service in closing the wide gap that opened up in the late 1970s as orthodox Marxism and theories of the pre-crisis period – functionalism and Fabianism – found it difficult to make sense of the developments of the 1970s.[37]

If there is one major difference between the interpretation offered in this book and the DCS perspective it is that this book has tried to situate the democratic class-conflict within the framework of the policies of capitalist production as well as distribution. Thus it has viewed the success of the Swedish welfare state as closely related to the ability of social democracy and the labour movement to come to terms with the requirements of a capitalist economy. It is this production orientation of the successful welfare state that is often played down in the DCS perspective. Yet that is what has enabled class conflict to be worked out as a positive-sum game. The systemic nature of welfare capitalism and its constraints remain somewhat marginalized in this perspective.[38] On the other hand, the DCS approach is invaluable in any attempt to understand tripartism or corporatism, whether in respect of its fragility or the nature of its outcome.

## Summary and conclusions

In this book we have argued that the economic recession and the inflation of the 1970s weakened the credibility of the KWS very considerably. The crisis of confidence in the old model ended with the emergence of neo-conservative regimes, on the one hand, and social-corporatist regimes, on the other, as alternatives to the KWS. Both types of regime remain politically (that is to say, electorally) and economically viable. But they represent substantially different social policy choices and outcomes. However, the liberal-democratic polity and capitalist market economy have both acted as major influences of policy. Neo-conservative regimes have had to take into account the continuing popularity of universal social services and to moderate their ambition of retrenching social welfare, at least in the short run. Conversely, social-corporatist regimes have not been able to do more than to make a brave attempt at defending the welfare state. The experience of even the strongest of these regimes, Sweden and Austria, suggests that social programmes and services are unlikely to expand any further. Some restrictions of and reductions in social spending have taken place and the future portends a greater restraint on spending, to put it mildly. A relatively stable set of social programmes and services, rather along the lines of the 'maturity' thesis discussed above, is what is foreshadowed for the near future. However, given that these social welfare systems are located within a capitalist market economy – which is nothing if not dynamic and destabilizing – and that the political economy of welfare capitalism entails ideological and distributional conflict, then change is inevitable. And for the moment it is the forces of the right – those in favour of more market, more privatization, greater economic freedom and greater inequality – that seem to be ascendant even within the citadels of social corporatism.

It appears that in Sweden social democracy has been willing and able to defend the commitment not only to a high level of social welfare but also to full employment. This has helped in retaining electoral support. By contrast, Austrian social democracy has either been unwilling or unable to defend full employment. Unemployment rose in the 1980s, while politically the country drifted to the right. In Austria the right is a good deal stronger politically than it is in Sweden and further weakening of the welfare state remains a strong possibility. As far as Australia is concerned, social corporatism has done little to fight unemployment. After a brief period of promising advances in respect of social welfare and equity, the government has followed a course of action that is more pro-capitalist than pro-welfare.

In sum, if social corporatism represents the left tendency within contemporary welfare capitalism, it is also clear that in the post-crisis period the ideological spectrum has shifted to the right rather than to the left. Why this should be so is the great unanswered (perhaps unasked) question of contemporary politics.[39] The absence of a credible socialist programme on the left is certainly among the contextual factors which lend further support to the possibility of a rightward drift of welfare capitalism. Working-class and other forms of organized politics remain largely defensive and seek better terms within the confines of liberal capitalism. And it seems that as long as the lure of capitalism persists, with its limitless and therefore ever receding horizon of consumer goods and services (and there is no sign of any let-up in its attraction), then the prospects of qualitative change remain slight.

Meanwhile, however, the problem of social justice remains. And that is where the defence and improvement of the welfare state, that is to say, the institutionalized commitment to a national minimum for all and its more equitable and effective operation, come in. If we look at the pre-crisis welfare state as a combination of Keynesian and Beveridgian elements, it is clear that the Keynesian basis of fine-tuning the market economy in order to maintain full employment has been the chief casualty of the crisis. By contrast, the Beveridgian basis, that is, a set of universal and comprehensive social services as a major line of defence against poverty and as a means of maintaining national minimum standards, has stood up to the pressure from the right quite well. Clearly it is this core of the welfare state and its continuing popularity that must be considered as the most valuable legacy of the pre-crisis welfare state. Even where the working-class movement and the parties of the left have proved weak and ineffective (for example, in Thatcherite Britain) or where they have been virtually non-existent (for example, in Reagan's United States) the electorate has been firm (as have many interest groups and organizations) in its resistance to the encroachment on social rights. What the best social-corporatist regimes, such as Sweden, have shown is that a combination of industrial and parliamentary struggle for the social rights of welfare can succeed in defending the welfare state in a way not possible without linking the interests of the non-propertied masses in the workplace and in society at large.

But it is also clear that 'corporatism' is not a panacea. It decides nothing. It is both a form and a moment in the democratic struggle between the interests of the propertied and the non-propertied sections of the population. Its outcome depends on a host of factors connected with the state of civil society. Indeed, as Canada and to a lesser extent even Britain and the United States show, parliamentary and electoral politics in themselves have considerable potential for the defence of social rights, especially universal social programmes. Compared with social corporatism, however, electoral and interest-group politics remain reactive rather than proactive. The politics of welfare in the United States show this quite clearly. What is lacking is the ability to counterpose effective solidaristic policies against the 'divide and rule' policy of privatization and the selective retrenchment of social welfare.

Finally, we have reviewed three different interpretations of the state of the welfare state since the mid-1970s: irreversibility, maturity, and the changing welfare mix. We have argued that none of these three does justice to the changes taking place under neo-conservative regimes or to the struggle waged by social-corporatist regimes in defence of the welfare state. In particular, these perspectives either misunderstand or fail to consider adequately the role of class interests, ideology and stratification. A great deal has been written contesting the neo-conservative claim about the adverse effects on the economy of social expenditure and high taxation and the claim about the magical effects of supply-side economics.[40] However useful such exercises may have been in the 1970s and early 1980s, they now appear increasingly 'academic'. What the post-crisis period has made amply clear is that the New Right and its policies are, above all and unashamedly, ideological and interest-oriented. The crisis of the KWS has provided the occasion as well as the justification for restratifying welfare capitalism within the limits of electoral and other political constraints. The unfolding of policies in the United States and the United Kingdom has made it clear that the chief concern of neo-conservatives is not simply to ensure profitability or to reduce the deficit. It is also and above all to redistribute power and privilege upwards and to establish the ideological hegemony of the right, weakened during the halcyon days of post-war welfare capitalism.

True, given the constraints of a privately owned market economy and a liberal-democratic polity, the scope for radical change within welfare capitalism – whether towards the right or the left – seems somewhat limited. Yet the relationship between class, politics and ideology suggests that the range of social policy orientations which directly or indirectly inform the practice of government in Western industrial countries has widened a good deal during the 'post-crisis' period.

What importance we accord to the observable differences in government policies and their outcome in, say, the United States and Sweden or in the United Kingdom and Austria depends on the level at which analysis is pitched as well as on our value judgement. As the three views of the welfare state reviewed earlier imply in different ways, it could be that the stakes are not high in the game of choice and change in social policy in capitalist democracies today. But in the context of the high standards and values of social progress that have come to be accepted as the norm in advanced industrial societies – itself a valuable legacy of the period since the Second World War – the relatively 'modest' differences with respect to deprivation, insecurity and human indignity cannot be dismissed as insignificant. Seen as mediating the relationship between production and distribution, or, more generally, between economic and social objectives, social welfare policy in some form or other remains central to modern industrial society. It is the variation around this central institution and the causes and consequences of the variation in policy that merit closer attention in this post-crisis period of divergence.

## Notes and references

1. See Carson and Kerr (1988); 'Labour's Winter of Content', *The Economist* (18 July 1987).
2. See, for example, LeGrand and Winter (1987: 148); Ruggles and O'Higgins (1987: 187); Myles (1988: 78–9); and Therborn (1984: 26–9, 37). More recently Therborn and Roebroek (1986) concede that the welfare state can be, and is being, reversed through the interaction between neo-conservative policy and social stratification.
3. For example, it varies from the latent and mild functionalism of Therborn's (1984: 26–9) analysis in terms of evolutionary societal trends to the more explicit functionalism of Offe (1984: 153). See also Gough (1979: 136–41).
4. Heclo (1981: 386–7).
5. Heclo (1981: 386–7, 403–4).
6. Heclo (1981: 403).
7. Heclo (1986: 59).
8. Klein and O'Higgins (1988: 204).
9. Klein and O'Higgins (1988: 204).
10. Klein and O'Higgins (1988: 205).
11. Myles (1988: 81).
12. See, for example, Rein and Rainwater (1986); Rose (1986).
13. See, for example, Johnson (1987: 55–63, 181–4).
14. Rose (1986: 13–14).
15. Rose and Shiratori (1986: 11).
16. Rein and Rainwater (1986: 203).
17. Rein and Rainwater (1986: viii).
18. Titmuss (1958).
19. Rose (1986: 36).
20. Rose (1986: 15).
21. Judge (1987: 16).
22. Judge (1987: 26).
23. Judge (1987: 26).
24. Judge (1987: 26–7). See also Harding (1987).
25. See Rose (1986: 22–4).
26. See Johnson (1987: ch. 4, *passim*) and Harding (1989).
27  See Lee Bawden and Palmer (1984: 211); Salamon (1984: 272–4, 284; Gronbjerg (1983: 786–9).
28. For an approach which does consider the normative aspects of pluralism, see Judge (1987: 27–32).
29. See, for example, Deacon (1983: Introduction and Conclusion); Held and Keane (1984); and Kerans *et al.* (1987). See also George (1985) for a critique of one-dimensional ideologies of welfare for not distinguishing between statist and non-statist traditions in socialist thought.
30. OECD (1985b: 21).
31. Johnson (1987: 112–15).

32. See, for example, Furniss and Tilton (1977): ch. 7; Gronbjerg *et al.* (1978: chs 1–4).
33. Korpi (1983); Stephens (1979); Esping-Andersen and Korpi (1984); Esping-Andersen (1985).
34. See note 33.
35. See, for example, Korpi (1983: 226–7); Esping-Andersen (1985: 245).
36. Korpi (1980); Esping-Andersen (1985); Pontusson (1984).
37. See Lee and Raban (1988: esp. ch. 5) for an appraisal of this perspective ('realist') in the context of Fabian and Marxist orthodoxies.
38. See Pontusson (1984); Przeworski (1985: ch. 1).
39. The crisis of the 1970s and its aftermath has certainly dealt a body blow to left-wing idealism and revolutionary aspirations. However, history may yet surprise us with a left turn in the future. But if historical inevitability is set aside, then it is anybody's guess as to who shall have the 'last laugh'.
40. See, for example, Cameron (1982); and Kuttner (1984). For a recent example, see Block (1987).

# Appendix 1

# 'Welfare state': the problem of definition

The 'ideal-type' approach to the welfare state employed in this book (Chapter 2, pages 18–19) differs from the positivist approach which sees the welfare state as more or less 'developed' in terms of levels of social expenditure (that is, 'welfare effort'[1]). It also differs in emphasis from those approaches which argue that welfare states cannot simply be seen in quantitative terms as more or less developed but must be seen as varying according to such characteristics as full employment, universality of programmes and redistributive financing[2] – characteristics associated with various political ideologies, for example social democracy.

However, if there are only different types of welfare state regime then the question must be asked what it is that makes them 'welfare state' regimes in the first place, that is, what distinguishes them from those regimes which are not welfare states. In other words, the question of *variation around a theme* demands that the nature of the *theme* be identified first. This is what we have tried to do with our ideal-type of the post-war welfare state. As with all typologies, this involves both a qualitative and a quantitative dimension. While it is perfectly logical to see social policy as varying across political regimes, it is somewhat misleading, in my view, to use the term 'social policy' as almost interchangeably with 'welfare state'.[3] 'Social policy', I would submit, is a generic concept whereas the 'welfare state' has a fairly specific historical (post-war) and policy ('institutional') connotation which cannot be ignored.

A distinctive feature of our definition of the welfare state is that it includes the objectives and policies of full employment. This is a departure from the approach adopted by many political scientists and sociologists. Flora and Heidenheimer's discussion of the changing characteristics of the welfare state provides a good example.[4] Indeed, it is remarkable that Flora and Heidenheimer's book, whose subject matter is the development of the welfare state in Europe and North America and which appeared at a time when unemployment throughout the Western world had reached levels unprecedented since the 1940s, scarcely mentions unemployment policies and full employment although it examines unemployment insurance in some detail. Heclo, writing in the same volume, provides an exception.[5] He at least identifies full employment policies as a feature of the post-war welfare state. This is in keeping with our own historically specific view of the post-war welfare state which was the object of the neo-conservative attack of the 1970s. Full-employment policies, quite apart from their role as a form of income-maintenance policy, were an important target of the neo-conservative attack on the Keynesian underpinnings of the welfare state. For this work, concerned as it is with the crisis of the welfare state in the 1970s and its aftermath seen as a part of the ongoing class struggle between workers and capitalists, the question of full employment is crucial. Let us concede, however, that in the last analysis all definitions and typologies are based on judgments about 'significance'. Our own definition is no exception.[6]

## Notes and references

1. See Wilensky (1975).
2. Esping-Andersen (1985).
3. See, for example, Esping-Andersen (1985: 224, 230–4). For other classifications of welfare regimes, see Furniss and Tilton (1977); Jones (1985).
4. Flora and Heidenheimer (1981).
5. Heclo (1981).
6. For a useful overview of the problems of studying the welfare state, see Alber *et al.* (1987).

# Appendix 2

# Tables

**Table 1**   Rate of unemployment, 1970–88 (percentage of labour force)

|      | Australia | Austria | Canada | Sweden | United Kingdom | United States | OECD |
|------|-----------|---------|--------|--------|----------------|---------------|------|
| 1970 | 1.6 | 1.1 | 5.7 | 1.2 | 2.4 | 5.0 | 3.4 |
| 1971 | 1.9 | 1.0 | 6.2 | 2.1 | 2.9 | 6.0 | 3.7 |
| 1972 | 2.6 | 1.0 | 6.2 | 2.2 | 3.1 | 5.6 | 3.9 |
| 1973 | 2.3 | 0.9 | 5.5 | 2.0 | 2.1 | 4.9 | 3.5 |
| 1974 | 2.7 | 1.1 | 5.3 | 1.6 | 2.2 | 5.6 | 3.9 |
| 1975 | 4.9 | 1.5 | 6.9 | 1.3 | 3.6 | 8.3 | 5.4 |
| 1976 | 4.7 | 1.5 | 7.1 | 1.3 | 4.8 | 7.7 | 5.5 |
| 1977 | 5.6 | 1.4 | 8.1 | 1.5 | 5.2 | 7.0 | 5.5 |
| 1978 | 6.3 | 1.7 | 8.3 | 1.8 | 5.1 | 6.1 | 5.5 |
| 1979 | 6.2 | 1.7 | 7.4 | 1.7 | 4.5 | 5.8 | 5.4 |
| 1980 | 6.0 | 1.5 | 7.5 | 1.6 | 6.1 | 7.2 | 6.2 |
| 1981 | 5.7 | 2.1 | 7.5 | 2.1 | 9.1 | 7.6 | 7.0 |
| 1982 | 7.1 | 3.1 | 11.1 | 2.7 | 10.4 | 9.7 | 8.4 |
| 1983 | 9.9 | 3.7 | 11.9 | 2.9 | 11.3 | 9.6 | 8.9 |
| 1984 | 8.9 | 3.8 | 11.3 | 2.6 | 11.5 | 7.5 | 8.5 |
| 1985 | 8.2 | 3.6 | 10.5 | 2.4 | 11.7 | 7.1 | 8.4 |
| 1986 | 8.0 | 3.1 | 9.6 | 2.2 | 11.8 | 7.0 | 8.3 |
| 1987 | 8.1 | 3.7 | 8.9 | 1.9 | 10.4 | 6.2 | 7.9 |
| 1988 | 7.1 | 3.5 | 7.8 | 1.6 | 8.2 | 5.5 | 7.3 |

*Sources*: OECD (1988a: 187); OECD (1989: 189).

**Table 2**  Economic growth, 1970–88 (percentage change in real GNP/GDP)

|       | Australia | Austria | Canada | Sweden | United Kingdom | United States | OECD |
|-------|-----------|---------|--------|--------|----------------|---------------|------|
| 1970  | −6.3      | 6.4     | 2.6    | 6.5    | 2.2            | −0.3          | 2.7  |
| 1971  | 5.9       | 5.1     | 5.8    | 0.9    | 1.7            | 2.8           | 3.5  |
| 1972  | 3.9       | 6.2     | 5.7    | 2.3    | 3.2            | 5.0           | 5.1  |
| 1973  | 5.9       | 4.9     | 7.7    | 4.0    | 7.1            | 5.2           | 5.8  |
| 1974  | 1.4       | 3.9     | 4.4    | 3.2    | −1.8           | −0.5          | 0.6  |
| 1975  | 2.6       | −0.4    | 2.6    | 2.6    | −1.1           | −1.3          | −0.5 |
| 1976  | 3.6       | 4.6     | 6.2    | 1.1    | 2.9            | 4.9           | 4.7  |
| 1977  | 0.8       | 4.4     | 3.6    | −1.6   | 2.2            | 4.7           | 3.7  |
| 1978  | 3.4       | 0.5     | 4.6    | 1.8    | 3.6            | 5.3           | 4.2  |
| 1979  | 3.4       | 4.7     | 3.9    | 4.0    | 2.7            | 2.5           | 3.2  |
| 1980  | 2.0       | 3.0     | 1.5    | 1.4    | −2.4           | −0.2          | 1.1  |
| 1981  | 3.1       | −0.1    | 3.7    | −0.3   | −1.2           | 1.9           | 1.6  |
| 1982  | 0.2       | 1.1     | −3.2   | 0.8    | 1.6            | −2.5          | −0.5 |
| 1983  | 0.2       | 2.2     | 3.2    | 2.4    | 3.3            | 3.6           | 2.7  |
| 1984  | 6.7       | 1.4     | 6.3    | 4.0    | 2.6            | 6.8           | 4.9  |
| 1985  | 5.5       | 2.8     | 4.3    | 2.1    | 3.6            | 3.0           | 3.2  |
| 1986  | 1.8       | 1.7     | 3.3    | 1.2    | 3.3            | 2.9           | 2.8  |
| 1987  | 4.4       | 1.3     | 3.9    | 2.8    | 4.5            | 2.9           | 3.1  |
| 1988  | 3.8       | 4.2     | 4.5    | 2.1    | 3.7            | 3.9           | 4.1  |

*Sources*: OECD (1988a: 170); OECD (1989: 172).

**Table 3**   Consumer prices, 1970–88 (percentage change)

|      | Australia | Austria | Canada | Sweden | United Kingdom | United States | OECD |
|------|-----------|---------|--------|--------|----------------|---------------|------|
| 1970 | 3.9  | 4.4 | 3.4  | 7.0  | 6.4  | 5.8  | 5.8  |
| 1971 | 6.1  | 4.7 | 2.8  | 7.4  | 9.4  | 4.3  | 5.2  |
| 1972 | 5.8  | 6.3 | 4.8  | 6.0  | 7.1  | 3.3  | 4.7  |
| 1973 | 9.5  | 7.6 | 7.6  | 6.7  | 9.2  | 6.2  | 7.8  |
| 1974 | 15.1 | 9.5 | 10.9 | 9.9  | 16.0 | 11.1 | 13.4 |
| 1975 | 15.1 | 8.4 | 10.8 | 9.8  | 24.2 | 9.1  | 11.3 |
| 1976 | 13.5 | 7.3 | 7.5  | 10.3 | 16.5 | 5.7  | 8.7  |
| 1977 | 12.3 | 5.5 | 8.0  | 11.4 | 15.8 | 6.5  | 8.9  |
| 1978 | 7.9  | 3.6 | 8.9  | 10.0 | 8.3  | 7.6  | 7.8  |
| 1979 | 9.1  | 3.7 | 9.2  | 7.2  | 13.4 | 11.3 | 9.7  |
| 1980 | 10.2 | 6.4 | 10.2 | 13.7 | 18.0 | 13.5 | 13.0 |
| 1981 | 9.6  | 6.8 | 12.5 | 12.1 | 11.9 | 10.3 | 10.5 |
| 1982 | 11.1 | 5.4 | 10.8 | 8.6  | 8.6  | 6.1  | 7.7  |
| 1983 | 10.1 | 3.3 | 5.8  | 8.9  | 4.6  | 3.2  | 5.3  |
| 1984 | 3.9  | 5.6 | 4.3  | 8.0  | 5.0  | 4.3  | 5.2  |
| 1985 | 6.8  | 3.2 | 4.0  | 7.4  | 6.1  | 3.5  | 4.5  |
| 1986 | 9.1  | 1.7 | 4.2  | 4.3  | 3.4  | 1.9  | 2.6  |
| 1987 | 8.5  | 1.4 | 4.4  | 4.2  | 4.2  | 3.7  | 3.2  |
| 1988 | 7.2  | 2.0 | 4.0  | 5.8  | 4.9  | 4.1  | 3.8  |

*Sources*: OECD (1988a: 180); OECD (1989: 182).

**Table 4** G ·neral government financial balances, 1970–87 (percentage of GDP/GNP)

|  | Australia | Austria | Canada | Sweden | United Kingdom | United States | OECD (17 countries)* |
|---|---|---|---|---|---|---|---|
| 1970 | 2.9 | 1.0 | 0.9 | 4.4 | 2.5 | −1.0 | 0.1 |
| 1971 | 2.4 | 1.5 | 0.1 | 5.2 | 1.4 | −1.8 | −0.6 |
| 1972 | 2.2 | 2.0 | 0.1 | 4.4 | −1.8 | −0.3 | −0.5 |
| 1973 | −0.2 | 1.3 | 1.0 | 4.1 | −3.4 | −0.6 | 0.1 |
| 1974 | 2.4 | 1.3 | 1.9 | 1.9 | −3.8 | −0.3 | −0.5 |
| 1975 | −0.6 | −2.5 | −2.4 | 2.7 | −4.7 | −4.1 | −3.9 |
| 1976 | −3.0 | −3.7 | −1.7 | 4.5 | −4.9 | −2.2 | −2.8 |
| 1977 | −0.7 | −2.4 | −2.4 | 1.7 | −3.4 | −1.0 | −2.1 |
| 1978 | −2.2 | −2.8 | −3.1 | −0.5 | −4.2 | −0.0 | −2.3 |
| 1979 | −2.2 | −2.4 | −2.0 | −3.0 | −3.3 | 0.5 | −1.9 |
| 1980 | −1.6 | −1.7 | −2.8 | −3.7 | −3.5 | 1.3 | −2.5 |
| 1981 | −0.7 | −1.8 | −1.5 | −4.9 | −2.8 | −1.0 | −2.8 |
| 1982 | −0.5 | −3.4 | −5.9 | −6.3 | −2.5 | −3.5 | −4.1 |
| 1983 | −4.1 | −4.0 | −6.9 | −5.0 | −3.4 | −3.8 | −4.2 |
| 1984 | −3.3 | −2.6 | −6.6 | −2.6 | −3.9 | −2.8 | −3.5 |
| 1985 | −3.1 | −2.5 | −7.0 | −3.8 | −2.9 | −3.3 | −3.4 |
| 1986 | −2.5 | −3.5 | −5.5 | −0.7 | −2.7 | −3.5 | −3.4 |
| 1987 | −0.6 | −4.1 | −4.6 | 4.1 | −1.5 | −2.3 | −2.2 |

*1987 figure for 18 countries.

*Sources*: OECD (1988a: 182); OECD (1989: 184).

**Table 5** Socio-economic indicators, 1975–84

| | Annual average unemployment (%) | | Annual average GDP growth (%) | | Annual average change in consumer prices (%) | | Annual average budget balance (% of GDP) | |
|---|---|---|---|---|---|---|---|---|
| | 1975–9 | 1980–4 | 1975–9 | 1980–4 | 1975–9 | 1980–4 | 1975–9 | 1980–4 |
| Austria | 1.9 | 3.2 | 2.7 | 1.6 | 5.7 | 5.5 | −2.7 | −2.5 |
| Sweden | 1.9 | 2.8 | 1.5 | 1.6 | 9.7 | 10.2 | −2.5 | −4.4 |
| United Kingdom | 5.4 | 10.7 | 2.0 | 0.6 | 15.6 | 9.6 | −4.0 | −3.2 |
| United States | 6.9 | 8.1 | 3.3 | 2.0 | 8.0 | 7.5 | −1.4 | −2.5 |
| OECD Europe | 5.4 | 9.8 | 2.7 | 1.1 | 11.0 | 10.5 | −3.3 | −4.3 |

*Sources*: Calculated from OECD (1984a) and OECD (1987a).

**Table 6** Average rates of unemployment, 1960–86 (percentage of labour force)

|  | 1960–7 | 1968–73 | 1974–9 | 1980–6 |
|---|---|---|---|---|
| Australia | 1.9 | 2.0 | 5.0 | 7.6 |
| Austria | 2.0 | 1.4 | 1.6 | 3.3 |
| Canada | 4.8 | 5.4 | 7.2 | 9.8 |
| Sweden | 1.6 | 2.2 | 1.9 | 2.8 |
| United Kingdom | 1.5 | 2.4 | 4.2 | 10.1 |
| United States | 5.0 | 4.6 | 6.7 | 7.8 |
| OECD | 3.1 | 3.4 | 5.2 | 7.8 |

*Source*: OECD (1988b: 39).

**Table 7** Nature and incidence of taxation (c.1985)

| | Total tax receipts as a percentage of GDP* | Personal income taxes as a percentage of total taxes | Social security tax as a percentage of total taxes | | Marginal tax rates (%) on average wages† | Top marginal rate (%) of income tax‡ |
|---|---|---|---|---|---|---|
| | | | Employee | Employer | | |
| Australia | 30 (28) | 46.7 | – | – | 47.3 | 55 |
| Austria | 42 (39) | 23.8 | 14.3 | 16.7 | 54.5 | 62 |
| Canada | 33 (32) | 36.4 | 6.1 | 9.1 | 34.1 | 52 |
| Sweden | 51 (44) | 37.3 | – | 23.5 | 62.0 | 77 |
| United Kingdom | 38 (35) | 26.3 | 7.9 | 7.9 | 43.9 | 60 |
| United States | 29 (29) | 34.5 | 10.3 | 17.2 | 40.9 | 38 |

* Figures in parentheses are for 1975.
† Allowing for direct taxes at all levels of government, social security contributions and tax concessions.
‡ Excluding social security contributions.

*Sources:* Calculated from Hagemann *et al.* (1988: 208) and McKee (1987–8: 33).

**Table 8**   Male–female wage differences, *c*.1980

| | Female wage as a percentage of male wage (all sectors) | Female earnings as a percentage of male earnings* |
|---|---|---|
| Australia | 86.0† | NA |
| Austria | 77.6 | NA |
| Canada | 63.3 | NA |
| Norway | NA | 65.3 |
| Sweden | 80.7 | 72.1 |
| United Kingdom | 65.7 | 53.2 |
| United States | 59.1 | 60.1 |

\* Average monthly earnings of full-time workers in manufacturing.
† Adult wages in non-agricultural activities. Calculated from ILO (1984).

*Sources*: United Nations (1985); ILO (1984).

**Table 9**   Family income, by family type, *c*.1980 (salary plus cash benefits less income taxes and contributions, as a percentage of the net average production worker's wage)

| | Family Type | | | | |
|---|---|---|---|---|---|
| | (1) | (2) | (3) | (4) | (5) |
| Australia | 50.0 | 78.8 | 79.7 | 64.3 | 269.8 |
| Canada | 52.2 | 75.9 | 73.0 | 55.8 | 289.8 |
| Sweden | 93.8 | 123.1 | 122.6 | 116.5 | 258.1 |
| United Kingdom | 51.7 | 83.0 | 80.9 | 65.3 | 324.3 |
| United States | 54.9 | 100.8 | 92.2 | 65.6 | 260.3 |

(1) Female-headed; single parent not in labour force; two children.
(2) Female-headed; single parent employed at half average wage, irregular employment; two children.
(3) Two-parent; one earner, employed at half average wage, irregular employment; two children.
(4) Two-parent; one earner, unemployed for 13 months; two children.
(5) Two-parent; two earners; one earner employed at twice the average wage and one at the average wage; two children.

*Source*: Kamerman and Kahn (1982).

**Table 10** Percentage of population in poverty (standardized definition)

|  | Early 1970s* | c.1980† |
|---|---|---|
| Australia | 8.0 | NA |
| Austria | NA | NA |
| Norway | 5.0 | 4.8 |
| Sweden | 3.5 | 5.0 |
| Canada | 11.0 | 12.1 |
| Britain | 7.5 | 8.8 |
| USA | 13.0 | 16.9 |

\* Persons in households with less than two-thirds of average disposable income.
† Persons in households with disposable income below half of the median for all households.

*Sources*: \*OECD (1976b: 27, 66); †Ringen (1987: 260).

# Bibliography

Abramovitz, M. (1986), 'The privatization of the welfare state: a review', *Social Work*, July/August.

Albage, L. (1986), 'Recent trends in collective bargaining in Sweden: An employer's view', *International Labour Review*, 125(1).

Alber, J., Esping-Andersen, G. and Rainwater, L. (1987), 'Studying the welfare state: Issues and queries' in M. Dierkes, H. N. Weiler and A. B. Antal (eds), *Comparative Policy Research* (Gower, Aldershot).

Apple, N. (1980), 'The rise and fall of full employment capitalism', *Studies in Political Economy*, 4.

Armitage, A. (1988), *Social Welfare in Canada*, 2nd edn (McClelland and Stewart, Toronto).

Banting, K. G. (1986), 'The state and economic interests: An introduction' in Keith G. Banting (ed.), *The State and Economic Interests* (University of Toronto Press, Toronto).

Banting, K. G. (1987), 'The welfare state and inequality in the 1980s', *Canadian Review of Sociology and Anthropology*, 24(3).

Barry, N. (1987), *The New Right* (Croom Helm, London).

Beilharz, P. (1986), 'The Australian left: Beyond labourism?' in R. Miliband *et al.* (eds), *The Socialist Register 1985/86* (Merlin Press, London).

Bell, W. (1987), *Contemporary Social Welfare*, 2nd edn (Macmillan, New York).

Bercuson, D., Granatstein, J. L. and Young, W. R. (1986), *Sacred Trust? Brian Mulroney and the Conservative Party in Power* (Double-day, Toronto).

Block, F. (1987), 'Rethinking the political economy of the welfare state' in F. Block, R. A. Cloward, B. Ehrenreich and F. F. Piven, *The Mean Season* (Pantheon Books, New York).

Bosanquet, N. (1983), *After the New Right* (Heinemann, London).

Bradbury, B., Rossiter, C. and Vipond, J. (1986), 'Housing Costs and Poverty', *The Australian Quarterly*, 58(1).

Briggs, A. (1967), 'The welfare state in historical perspective' in C. I. Schottland (ed.), *The Welfare State* (Harper & Row, New York).

Brosnan, P. and Wilkinson, F. (1987), *Cheap Labour: Britain's False Economy* (Low Pay Unit, London).

Brown, M. K. (1988), 'The segmented welfare system: Distributive conflict and retrenchment in the United States, 1968–1984' in M. K. Brown (ed.), *Remaking the Welfare State* (Temple University Press, Philadelphia).

Browne, P. (1987), '1981–1986: Poverty on the rise', *Australian Society*, April.

Busch, G., Münz, R., Nowotny, H., Reithofer, H., Schmidl, H. and Wintersberger, M. (1986), 'Development and prospects of the Austrian welfare state' in E. Øyen (ed.), *Comparing Welfare States and Their Futures* Gower, Aldershot).

Butschek, F. (1982), 'Welfare' in S. w. Arndt (ed.), *The Political Economy of Austria* (American Enterprise Institute of Public Policy Research, Washington, DC).

Calvert, J. (1984), *Government, Limited* (Canadian Centre for Policy Alternatives, Ottawa).

Cameron, D. R. (1982), 'On the limits of the public economy', *Annals of the American Academy of Political and Social Science*, 459, January.

Campling, J. (1986), 'Social administration digest', *Journal of Social Policy* 15(3).

Campling, J. (1988), 'Social policy digest', *Journal of Social Policy*, 17(4).

Campling, J. (1989a), 'Social policy digest', *Journal of Social Policy*, 18(1).

Campling, J. (1989b), 'Social policy digest', *Journal of Social Policy*, 18 (3).

Canada (1984), *A New Direction for Canada* (Department of Finance, Ottawa).

Canadian Council on Social Development (1988), 'Budget legacy: Lower income, higher taxes', *Overview*, 5(3).

Carmichael, J. and Plowman, K. (1985), 'Income provision in old age', *Australian Economic Review*, 71, Spring.

Carroll, W. K. (1984), 'The solidarity coalition' in W. Magnusson, W. K. Carroll, C. Doyle, M. Langer and R. B. J. Walker (eds), *The New Reality: The Politics of Restraint in British Columbia* (New Star Books, Vancouver).

Carson, E. and Kerr, H. (1988), 'Social welfare down under', *Critical Social Policy*, 23.

Cass, B. (1987), 'Family policy and the tax/transfer system: A longer-term agenda and priorities for reform' in P. Saunders and A. Jamrozik (eds), *Social Welfare in the Late 1980s* (Social Welfare Research Centre, Kensington, NSW).

Castles, F. G. (1985), *The Working Class and Welfare* (Allen & Unwin, Sydney).

Castles, F. G. (1987), 'Trapped in an historical cul-de-sac: The prospects for welfare reform in Australia' in P. Saunders and A. Jamrozik (eds.)

*Social Welfare in the late 1980s* (Social Welfare Research Centre, Kensington, NSW).

Chapman, B. (1985), 'Continuity and change: Labour market programs and education expenditure', *Australian Economic Review*, 71, Spring.

Chorney, H. and Molloy, A. (1988), 'The myth of tax reform: The Mulroney government's tax changes' in A. B. Gollner and D. Salee (eds), *Canada Under Mulroney* (Véhicule Press, Montreal).

Conference of Socialist Economists (CSE) (1980), *The Alternative Economic Strategy* (CSE Books, London).

Courtney, J. C. (1988), 'Reinventing the brokerage wheel: The Tory success in 1984' in H. Penniman (ed.), *Canada at the Polls, 1984* (American Enterprise Institute, Washington, DC).

Cripps, F. (1981), 'The British crisis – can the left win?', *New Left Review* 128.

Deacon, B. (1983), *Social Policy and Socialism* (Pluto Press, London).

Deacon, B. (1985–6), 'Strategies for welfare: East and West Europe', *Critical Social Policy*, 14.

Economic Council of Canada (1984), *Steering the Course, Twenty-first Annual Review* (Supply and Services, Ottawa).

Einhorn, E. and Logue, J. (1982), *Welfare States in Hard Times* (Kent Popular Press, Kent, Ohio).

Elliot, G. (1982), 'The social policy of the New Right' in M. Sawer (ed.), *Australia and the New Right* (Allen & Unwin, Sydney).

Esping-Andersen, G. (1985), 'Power and distributional regimes', *Politics and Society*, 14(2).

Esping-Andersen, G. and Korpi, W. (1984), 'Social policy as class politics in post-war capitalism: Scandinavia, Austria and Germany' in J. H. Goldthorpe (ed.), *Order and Conflict in Contemporary Capitalism* (Oxford University Press, New York).

Ferguson, T. and Rogers, J. (1986), *Right Turn* (Hill and Wang, New York).

Ferris, P. (1985), 'Citizenship and the crisis of the welfare state' in P. Beau, J. Ferris and D. Whynes (eds), *In Defence of Welfare* (Tavistock, London).

Fjällström, H. (1986),'Recent trends in collective bargaining in Sweden (A Trade Unionist's Reply)', *International Labour Review*, 125(1).

Flora, P and Heidenheimer, A. J. (1981), 'The historical core and changing boundaries of the welfare state' in P. Flora and A. J. Heidenheimer (eds), *The Development of Welfare States in Europe and America* (Transaction Books, New Brunswick, NJ).

Frizzell, A. and Westell, A. (1985), *The Canadian General Election of 1984* (Carleton University Press, Ottawa).

Furniss, N. and Tilton, T. (1977), *The Case for the Welfare State* (Indiana University Press, Bloomington).

George, P. (1985), 'Towards a two-dimensional analysis of welfare ideologies', *Social Policy and Administration*, 19(1).

Gilbert, B. B. (1966), *The Evolution of National Insurance in Great Britain* (Michael Joseph, London).

Gilbert, N. (1983), *Capitalism and the Welfare State* (Yale University Press, New Haven, Conn.).

Glazer, N. (1971), 'The limits of social policy', *Commentary*, 52.

Gough, I. (1979), *The Political Economy of the Welfare State* (Macmillan, London).

Graycar, A. (ed.) (1983), *Retreat from the Welfare State* (Allen & Unwin, Sydney).

Gronbjerg, K. (1983), 'Private welfare: Its future in the welfare state', *American Behavioral Scientist*, 26(6).

Gronbjerg, K., Street, D. and Suttles, G. D. (1978), *Poverty and Social Change* (University of Chicago Press, Chicago).

Guest, D. (1985), *The Emergence of Social Security in Canada* (University of British Columbia Press, Vancouver).

Gwyn, W. B. and Rose, R. (eds) (1980), *Britain: Progress and Decline* (Macmillan, London).

Hagemann, R. P., Jones, B. R. and Montador, R. B. (1988), 'Tax reform in OECD countries', *OECD Economic Studies*, 10, Spring.

Harding, P. (1987), 'Beveridge's conception of welfare capitalism: DWS or IWS?', *Journal of International and Comparative Social Welfare*, 3(1–2), Spring/Fall.

Harding, P. (1989), 'Models of social welfare and gender equality: A comparative analysis', *Canadian Review of Social Policy*, 24, October.

Harrington, M. (1984), *The New American Poverty* (Penguin Books, New York).

Harrington, M. and Levinson, M. (1985), 'The perils of a dual economy', *Dissent*, Autumn.

Harrison, B. (1987), 'The impact of corporate restructuring on labour income', *Social Policy*, 18(2).

Harrison, M. L. (1984), 'Themes and objectives' in M. L. Harrison (ed.), *Corporatism and the Welfare State* (Gower, Aldershot).

Head, B. (1982), 'The New Right and welfare expenditures' in M. Sawer (ed.), *Australia and the New Right* (Allen & Unwin, Sydney).

Heclo, H. (1981), 'Toward a new welfare state?' in P. Flora and A. J. Heidenheimer (eds), *The Development of Welfare States in Europe and America* (Transaction Books, New Brunswick, NJ).

Heclo, H. (1986), 'Reaganism and the search for a public philosophy' in J. L. Palmer (ed.), *Perspectives on the Reagan Years* (The Urban Institute, Washington, DC).

Held, D. and Keane, J. (1984), 'Socialism and the limits of state action' in J. Curran (ed.), *The Future of the Left* (Polity Press, Cambridge).

Henning, R. (1984), 'Industrial policy or employment policy? Sweden's response to unemployment' in J. Richardson and R. Henning (eds), *Unemployment* (Sage, London).

Higgins, J. (1981), *States of Welfare* (Blackwell, Oxford).

Howe, B. (1987), ' "The welfare state": Reform, progress or retreat?' in P. Saunders and A. Jamrozik (eds), *Social Welfare in the late 1980s* (Social Welfare Research Centre, Kensington, NSW).

Hyde, M. and Deacon, B. (1986–7), 'Working-class opinion and welfare strategies', *Critical Social Policy*, 18.

Ilfe, J. (1987), 'Public opinion and welfare policy: Is there a crisis of legitimacy?' in P. Saunders and A. Jamrozik (eds), *Social Welfare in the Late 1980s* (Social Welfare Research Centre, Kensington, NSW).

International Labour Office (1984), *Yearbook of Labour Statistics 1984* (ILO, Geneva).

Jamrozik, A. (1987), 'Winners and losers in the welfare state' in P. Saunders and A. Jamrozik (eds), *Social Welfare in the Late 1980s*, (Social Welfare Research Centre, Kensington, NSW).

Jangenas, B. (1985), *The Swedish Approach to Labor Market Policy* (Swedish Institute, Uppsala).

Johnson, D. (1988), 'The measurement of poverty in Australia: 1981–82 and 1985–86', *Australian Economic Review*, 83, Spring.

Johnson, N. (1987), *The Welfare State in Transition* (Wheatsheaf Books, Brighton).

Jones, C. (1985), *Patterns of Social Policy* (Tavistock, London).

Jones, H. G. (1976), *Planning and Productivity in Sweden* (Croom Helm, London).

Judge, K. (1987), 'The British welfare state in transition' in R. R. Friedman, N. Gilbert and M. Scherer (eds), *Modern Welfare States* (New York University Press, New York).

Kaim-Caudle, P. R. (1973), *Comparative Social Policy and Social Security* (Martin Robertson, London).

Kamerman, S. B. and Kahn, A. J. (1982), 'Income transfers, work and the economic well-being of families with children: A comparative study', *International Social Security Review*, 35(3).

Kerans, P., Drover, G. and Williams, D. (1987), *Welfare and Worker Participation* (Macmillan, London).

Kesselman, M. (1986), 'Lyrical illusions or a socialism of governance: Whither French socialism?' in R. Miliband, J. Saville, M. Liebman and L. Panitch (eds), *The Socialist Register 1985–86* (Merlin Press, London).

King, D. S. (1987), *The New Right* (Macmillan, London).

Kirwin, B. (1986), 'Nielsen spending review defends CAP', *Perception*, 9(5).

Kitchen, B. (1986), 'The Marsh Report revisited', *Journal of Canadian Studies*, 21(2).

Klein, R. and O'Higgins, M. (1988), 'Defusing the crisis of the welfare state: A new interpretation' in T. R. Marmor and J. L. Mashaw (eds), *Social Security: Beyond the Rhetoric of Crisis* (Princeton University Press, Princeton, NJ).

Korpi, W. (1980), 'Social policy and distributional conflict in capitalist democracies', *West European Politics*, 3(3).

Korpi, W. (1983), *The Democratic Class Struggle* (Routledge, London).

Krieger, J. (1986), *Reagan, Thatcher and the Politics of Decline* (Polity Press, Cambridge).

Krieger, J. (1987), 'Social policy in the age of Reagan and Thatcher' in R.

Miliband, L. Panitch, and J. Saville (eds), *The Socialist Register 1987* (Merlin Press, London).

Kristol, I, (1971), 'Welfare: The best of intentions, the worst of results', *The Atlantic Monthly*, 228(2).

Kudrle. R. T. and Marmor, T. R. (1981), 'The Development of welfare states in North America' in P. Flora and A. J. Heidenheimer (eds), *The Development of Welfare States in Europe and America* (Transaction Books, New Brunswick, NJ).

Kuhnle, S. (1981), 'The growth of social insurance programs in Scandinavia: Outside influences and internal forces' in P. Flora and A. J. Heidenheimer (eds), *The Development of Welfare States in Europe and America* (Transaction Books, New Brunswick, NJ).

Kuttner, R. (1984) *The Economic Illusion* (Houghton Mifflin, Boston).

Labour Party Research Department (1985), *Breaking the Nation* (Pluto Press, London).

Lachapelle, G. (1988),'Between income security and family equalization' in A. B. Gollner and D. Salee (eds), *Canada under Mulroney* (Véhicule Press, Montreal).

Lee, P. and Raban, C. (1988), *Welfare Theory and Social Policy* (Sage, London).

Lee Bawden, D. and Palmer, J. L. (1984), 'Social policy: Challenging the welfare state' in J. L. Palmer and I. V. Sawhill (eds), *The Reagan Record* (The Urban Institute, Washington, DC).

LeGrand, J. and Winter, D. (1987), 'The middle classes and the defence of the British welfare state' in R. E Goodin and J. LeGrand (eds), *Not Only the Poor* (Allen & Unwin).

Leman, C. (1977), 'Patterns of policy development: Social security in the United States and Canada', *Public Policy*, 25.

Leman, C. (1980), *The Collapse of Welfare Reform* (MIT Press, Cambridge, Mass.).

Levitas, R. (ed.) (1985), *The Ideology of the New Right* (Polity Press, Cambridge).

Lipset, S. M. (1985), 'The elections, the economy and public opinion: 1984', *PS: The Journal of the American Political Science Association*, 18(1).

Loney, M. (1986), *The Politics of Greed* (Pluto Press, London).

Lubove, R. (1968), *The Struggle for Social Security* (Harvard University Press, Cambridge, Mass.).

Luther, K. R. (1987), 'Austria's future and Waldheim's past: The significance of the 1986 elections', *West European Politics*, 10(3).

Magnusson, W., Carroll, W. K., Doyle, C., Langer, M. and Walker, R. B. J. (eds) (1984), 'Introduction' in W. Magnusson *et al.* (eds), *The New Reality: The Politics of Restraint in British Columbia* (New Star Books, Vancouver).

Maier, C. S. (1984), 'Preconditions for corporatism' in J. H. Goldthorpe (ed.), *Order and Conflict in Contemporary Capitalism* (Oxford University Press, Oxford).

Manning, I, (1985), 'Continuity and change in Australian economic policy: The social welfare services', *Australian Economic Review*, 71, Spring.

Marklund, S. (1988), *Paradise Lost? The Nordic Welfare States and the Recession 1975-1985* (Arkiv, Lund).

Martin, A. (1986), 'The politics of employment and welfare: National polities and international interdependence' in K. Banting (ed.), *The State and Economic Interests* (University of Toronto Press, Toronto).

McCallum, J. (1984), 'The assets test and the needy', *Australian Journal of Social Issues*, 19(3).

McDonald, D. (1988), 'A description of recent developments in the Australian economy in an historical context', *Australian Economic Review*, 81(1).

McIntyre, S. (1986), 'The short history of social democracy in Australia', *Thesis Eleven*, 15.

McKee, M. (1987-8), 'Paying the public sector's bills', *OECD Observer*, 149, December–January.

Micklewright, J. (1984), 'Male unemployment and the family expenditure survey 1972–80', *Oxford Bulletin of Economics and Statistics*, 46(1).

Miller, S. M. (1980), 'The eighties and the left: An American view' in R. Miliband and J. Saville (eds), *The Socialist Register 1980* (Merlin Press, London).

Miller, S. M. and Jenkins, M. (1987), 'Challenging the American welfare state' in Z. Ferge and S. M. Miller (eds), *Dynamics of Deprivation* (Gower, Aldershot).

Mills, G. B. (1984), 'The budget: A failure of discipline' in J. L. Palmer and I. V. Sawhill (eds), *The Reagan Record* (The Urban Institute, Washington, DC).

Mishra, R. (1984), *The Welfare State in Crisis* (Wheatsheaf Books, Brighton).

Mishra, R. (1986), 'Social analysis and the welfare state: Retrospect and prospect' in E. Øyen (ed.), *Comparing Welfare States and Their Futures* (Gower, Aldershot).

Moon, J. and Richardson, J. J. (1985), *Unemployment in the United Kingdom* (Gower, Aldershot).

Moon, M. and Sawhill, I.V. (1984), 'Family incomes: Gainers and losers' in J. L. Palmer and I. V. Sawhill (eds), *The Reagan Record* (The Urban Institute, Washington, DC).

Moscovitch, A. (1986), 'The welfare state since 1975', *Journal of Canadian Studies*, 21(2).

Moscovitch, A. (1988),'The Canada Assistance Plan' in K. A. Graham (ed.), *How Ottawa Spends 1988/89* (Carleton University Press, Ottawa).

Moynihan, D. P. (1969), 'The professors and the poor' in D. P. Moynihan (ed.), *On Understanding Poverty* (Basic Books, New York).

Münz, R. and Wintersberger, H. (1987), 'The making of the Austrian welfare state' in R. R. Friedman, N. Gilbert and M. Scherer (eds), *Modern Welfare States* (New York University Press, New York).

Myles, J. (1988), 'Decline or impasse? The current state of the welfare state', *Studies in Political Economy*, 26.

National Council of Welfare (1988), *Poverty Profile 1988* (Supply and Services Canada, Ottawa).

National Council of Welfare (1989), *Social Spending and the Next Budget* (Supply and Services Canada, Ottawa).

Navarro, V. (1985), 'The road ahead', *Monthly Review*, 37(3).

Nozick, R. (1974), *Anarchy, State and Utopia* (Basic Books, New York).

Nurick, J. (1987) (ed.) *Mandate to Govern* (Australian Institute for Public Policy, Perth).

OECD (1964), *General Statistics*, January (Paris).

OECD (1976a), *Economic Surveys: Canada*, June (Paris).

OECD (1976b), *Public Expenditure on Income Maintenance Programmes* (Paris).

OECD (1980), 'Incomes policy in theory and practice', *Economic Outlook: Occasional Studies*, July 1980.

OECD (1981), *Integrated Social Policy: A Review of the Austrian Experience* (Paris).

OECD (1982a), *Economic Surveys 1981–1982: Austria* (Paris).

OECD (1982b), *Economic Surveys: Canada*, June (Paris).

OECD (1982c), *Economic Surveys: 1981–1982 Sweden* (Paris).

OECD (1983), *Economic Surveys: 1982–1983 Austria* (Paris).

OECD (1984a), *Economic Outlook: Historical Statistics 1960–1982* (Paris).

OECD (1984b), *Economic Surveys 1983/1984: Canada* (Paris).

OECD (1985a), *Economic Surveys 1984/1985: Sweden* (Paris).

OECD (1985b), *Social Expenditure 1960–1990* (Paris).

OECD (1987a), *Economic Outlook 42*, December (Paris).

OECD (1987b), *Economic Surveys 1986/1987: Australia* (Paris).

OECD (1987c), *Economic Surveys 1986/1987: Sweden* (Paris).

OECD (1987d), *Revenue Statistics of OECD Member Countries 1965/86* (Paris).

OECD (1987–8), *The OECD Observer*, no. 149. December–January (Paris).

OECD (1988a), *Economic Outlook 43*, June (Paris).

OECD (1988b), *Economic Outlook: Historical Statistics 1960–1986* (Paris).

OECD (1988c), *Economic Surveys 1987/1988: Australia* (Paris).

OECD (1988d), *The OECD Observer*, no. 151, April–May (Paris).

OECD (1989), *Economic Outlook 45*, June (Paris).

Offe, C. (1984), 'Some contradictions of the modern welfare state' in C. Offe, *Contradictions of the Welfare State*, ed. J. Keane (MIT Press, Cambridge, Mass.).

O'Higgins, M. (1985), 'Inequality, redistribution and recession: The British experience, 1976–1982' *Journal of Social Policy*, 14(3).

Olsson, S. E. (1987), *Growth to Limits: The Western European Welfare States Since World War II: The Case of Sweden*, Reprint No. 176 (Swedish Institute for Social Research, Stockholm).

Palmer, J. L. and Sawhill, I. V. (1984a), 'Overview' in J. L. Palmer and

I. V. Sawhill (eds), *The Reagan Record* (The Urban Institute, Washington, DC).

Palmer, J. L. and Sawhill, I. V. (1984b), 'Summaries of Major Social Programs' (Appendix C) in J. L. Palmer and I. V. Sawhill (eds), *The Reagan Record* (The Urban Institute, Washington, DC).

Panitch, L. (1986), 'The tripartite experience' in K. Banting (ed.), *The State and Economic Interests* (University of Toronto Press, Toronto).

Panitch, L. and Swartz, D. (1985), *From Consent to Coercion: The Assault on Trade Union Freedoms* (Garamond Press, Toronto).

Parliament, J. (1987), 'Increases in long-term unemployment', *Canadian Social Trends*, Spring.

Perlin, G. (1988), 'Opportunity regained: The Tory victory in 1984' in H. Penniman, (ed.) *Canada at the Polls, 1984* (American Enterprise Institute, n.p.).

Piven, F. F. and Cloward, R. A. (1985), *The New Class War* (Pantheon Books, New York).

Piven, F. F. and Cloward, R. A. (1987), 'The Contemporary Relief Debate' in F. Block, R. A. Cloward, B. Ehrenreich and F. F. Piven (eds), *The Mean Season* (Pantheon Books, New York).

Pontusson, J. (1984), 'Behind and beyond social democracy in Sweden', *New Left Review*, 143.

Prince, M. J. (1985), 'Social policy in PC Year One', *Perception*, 9(1).

Prince, M. J. (1986a), 'Federal Budget '86: Social policy through the tax system', *Perception*, 9(4/5).

Prince, M. J. (1986b), 'The Mulroney agenda: A right turn for Ottawa?' in M. J. Prince (ed.), *How Ottawa Spends 1986–87* (Methuen, Toronto).

Przeworski, A. (1985), *Capitalism and Social Democracy* (Cambridge University Press, Cambridge).

Rein, M. and Rainwater, L. (1986), 'Introduction' in M. Rein and L. Rainwater (eds), *Public/Private Interplay in Social Protection* (M. E. Sharpe, Armonk, NY).

Rice, J. J. (1987), 'Restricting the safety net: Altering the national social security system' in M. J. Prince (ed.), *How Ottawa Spends 1987–88* (Methuen, Toronto).

Riches, G. (1987), 'Feeding Canada's poor: The rise of the food banks and the collapse of the public safety net' in J. S. Ismael (ed.), *The Canadian Welfare State* (University of Alberta Press, Edmonton).

Riddell, P. (1985), *The Thatcher Government* (Basil Blackwell, Oxford).

Ringen, S. (1987), *The Possibility of Politics* (Oxford University Press, New York).

Robinson, R. (1986), 'Restructuring the welfare state: An analysis of public expenditure, 1979/80–1984/85', *Journal of Social Policy*, 15(1).

Rose, R. (1986), 'Common goals but different roles: The state's contribution to the welfare mix' in R. Rose and R. Shiratori (eds), *The Welfare State East and West* (Oxford University Press, New York).

Rose, R. and Shiratori, R. (1986), 'Introduction' in R. Rose and R. Shiratori (eds), *The Welfare State East and West* (Oxford University Press, New York).

Ross, G. and Jenson, J. (1983), 'Crisis and France's "third way" ', *Studies in Political Economy*, 11.

Rothstein, B. (1987), 'Corporatism and reformism', *Acta Sociologica*, 30(3/4).

Ruggles, P. and O'Higgins, M. (1987), 'Retrenchment and the New Right' in M. Rein, G. Esping-Andersen and L. Rainwater (eds), *Stagnation and Renewal in Social Policy* (M. E. Sharpe, Armonk, NY).

Salamon, L. M. (1984), 'Nonprofit organizations' in J. L. Palmer and I. V. Sawhill, (eds), *The Reagan Record* (The Urban Institute, Washington DC).

Salamon, L. M. and Abramson, A. J. (1984), 'Governance: The politics of retrenchment' in J. L. Palmer and I. V. Sawhill (eds), *The Reagan Record* (The Urban Institute, Washington, DC).

Saunders, P. (1987a), 'An agenda for social security in the years ahead', *Australian Journal of Social Issues*, 22(2).

Saunders, P. (1987b), Past developments and future prospects for social security in Australia' in P. Saunders and A. Jamrozik (eds), *Social Welfare in the Late 1980s* (Social Welfare Research Centre, Kensington, NSW).

Saunders, P. and Whiteford, P. (1987), *Ending Child Poverty* (Social Welfare Research Centre, Kensington, NSW).

Schorr, A. L. (1986), *Common Decency* (Yale University Press, New Haven, Conn.).

Schott, K. (1987), 'The challenge to equity and fairness' in K. Coghill (ed.), *The New Right's Australian Fantasy* (Penguin Books, Ringwood, Vic.).

Sears, V. (1985), 'The buttery-smooth Conservatives' in A. Frizzell and A. Westell, *The Canadian General Election of 1984* (Carleton University Press, Ottawa).

Seidel, H. (1982), 'The Austrian economy: An overview' in S. W. Arndt (ed.), *The Political Economy of Austria* (American Enterprise Institute for Public Policy Research, Washington, DC).

Simeon, R. (1988), 'National reconciliation: The Mulroney government and federalism' in A. B. Gollner and D. Salée (eds), *Canada under Mulroney* (Véhicule Press, Montreal).

Social Planning Council of Metropolitan Toronto (1986), 'Welfare Benefits: An interprovincial comparison, 1985', *Social Infopac*, 5(1).

Stanbury, W. T. (1988), 'Privatization and the Mulroney Government, 1984–1988' in A. B. Gollner and D. Salée (eds), *Canada under Mulroney* (Véhicule Press, Montreal).

Steinfels, P. (1979), *The Neoconservatives* (Simon and Schuster, New York).

Stephens, J. D. (1979), *The Transition from Capitalism to Socialism* (Macmillan, London).

Stilwell, F. (1986), *The Accord and Beyond* (Pluto Press, Sydney).

Taylor-Gooby, P. (1985), *Public Opinion, Ideology and State Welfare* (Routledge, London).

Taylor-Gooby, P. (1987), 'The future of the British welfare state' (mimeo, University of Kent, Canterbury).

Ternowetsky, G. (1987), 'Controlling the deficit and a private sector led recovery' in J. S. Ismael (ed), *The Canadian Welfare State* (University of Alberta Press, Edmonton).

Therborn, G. (1984), 'The prospects of labour and the transformation of advanced capitalism', *New Left Review*, 145.

Therborn, G. (1986), *Why Some Peoples are More Unemployed than Others* (Verso, London).

Therborn, G. and Roebroek, J. (1986), 'The irreversible welfare state', *International Journal of Health Services*, 16(3).

Thurow, L. C. (1985), *The Zero-Sum Solution* (Simon & Schuster, New York).

Titmuss, R. M. (1958), *Essays on 'the Welfare State'* (Allen & Unwin, London).

United Nations (1985), *Economic Role of Women in E.C.E. Region: Developments 1975/85* (Geneva).

United States Bureau of the Census (1986), *Statistical Abstract of the United States 1987*, 107th edn (Washington, DC).

Vipond, J., Bradbury, B. and Encel, D. (1987), 'Unemployment and poverty: Measures of association', *Australian Bulletin of Labour*, 13(3).

Walters, P. (1985), 'Distributing decline', *Government and Opposition*, 20(3).

Weir, M., Skocpol, T. and Orloff, T. (1988), *The Politics of Social Policy in the United States* (Princeton University Press, Princeton, NJ).

Whitlam, G. (1985), *The Whitlam Government* (Penguin Books, Ringwood, Vic.).

Wilenski, P. (1980), 'Reform and its implementation: The Whitlam years in retrospect' in G. Evans and J. Reeves (eds), *Labor Essays 1980* (Drummond, Melbourne).

Wilensky, H. L. (1975), *The Welfare State and Equality* (University of California Press, Berkeley).

Wilson, V. S. (1988), 'What legacy? The Nielsen Task Force program review' in K. A. Graham (ed.), *How Ottawa Spends* (Carleton University Press, Ottawa).

Wolfe, D. A. (1985), 'The Tory agenda for economic renewal: A political overview' in *The Government's Agenda for Economic Renewal* (Canadian Centre for Policy Alternatives, Ottawa).

Zimbalist, S. E. (1987), 'A welfare state against the economic current: Sweden and the United States as contrasting cases', *International Social Work*, 30.

# Index